Structured around quotations and snip lifetime of leadership, *What Am I Supposed to Say?* offers readers a valuable opportunity to reflect on their own paths, principles, and priorities moving forward.

Dr. Dennis Huffman
Director, University Town Center
Prince George's Community College

After reading *What Am I Supposed to Say?* **I see applications for use in every aspect of my life**. Dr. gossom's nuggets of wisdom are explained with the kind of detail that allowed me to see my own 'learned lessons' and how they have 'transformed me.' From a child of reading age, through the oldest of adults this book is a MUST READ! Written at a necessary time ... thank you for sharing your gifts!

Karen Rones
Shalimar, FL

Unconventional is an accurate descriptor of *What Am I Supposed to Say?*. Some very excellent quotes.

Ricardo Soria
Chief, Retired
US Air Force

For me, *What Am I Supposed to Say?* is like a page of mirrors – I see myself at every page-turn ....

Dr. Cheryl Jones
Songwriter, Singer, Musician, Instructor
Jones & Company

What Am I Supposed to Say? is **a must read for leaders in all walks of life** who are not only looking to execute on tactics, but also transform their organization.

Foster Ware
Customer Experience Manager
Alabama Power

A fun quick read on how the develop personal power and leadership skills. In her book *Why Are They Following Me?* Dr. joyce gillie gossom provides practical ideas on how to become a better leader. Her colloquial style makes this for a quick read. She gives many great ideas that we can easily put into practice. "There is doing things right for approval and doing things right for results." "Eagles fly alone, ducks fly in formation." She suggests that you hire people who aren't like you. That is certainly an interesting thought. The reason being is that "I want to be surrounded by people who can do what I can't." I really loved this book. I read it in less than a day. Great job, Dr. joyce gillie gossom!!

Amazon Review
United States
April 9, 2020

Anyone wanting to make a positive difference in a business, institution, or organization can benefit from the sensible, practical and easy-to-follow advice joyce has packed into *Why Are They Following Me?.*"

Don Logan
Chairman, Retired
Time Warner Media & Communications

Why Are They Following Me? Because they want to be where you are. Because they believe in your vision and that you'll get there. **I can see this from a teaching perspective.** Students want to follow teachers who have a vision for them and teachers who let them in on the objective for the day and state the objective for the lesson. When a leader/teacher has a vision that has been articulated to students, they know that you have thought it through and will get them there. Students will learn how to work cooperatively. They will learn how to reduce fractions. They will learn to write, so that the message they are sending will be received and understood by the receivers. Thanks for giving me an opportunity to read your book.

Sharon Barfield Jenkins
Administrator, Retired
Chicago Public Schools

WHAT AM I SUPPOSED TO SAY?

An Unconventional Guide to Transformative Leadership

Dr. joyce gillie gossom

What Am I Supposed to Say?
An Unconventional Guide to Transformative Leadership

ISBN: 978-0-9890865-7-8

Best Gurl, inc.
PO Box 4235
Fort Walton Beach FL 32549

To my son, who transformed my life ... and my leadership.

CONTENTS

FOREWORD.. XI

INTRODUCTION XV

WHAT IS IT ABOUT RELATIONSHIPS? 1

WORK, WORK, WORK!.. 21

FAMILIES & FRIENDS 33

LOOKING FORWARD; LOOKING BACK 45

WHEN TIMES ARE HARD... 61

THE ART OF WAR ... ACCORDING TO SUN TZU 73

PEOPLE WHO LIVE IN GLASS HOUSES 91

IT'S ABOUT THE JOURNEY ... NOT THE DESTINATION 109

NOT SO FAMOUS LAST WORDS... 125

ABOUT THE AUTHOR 131

ACKNOWLEDGMENTS

Where do I begin to thank the people who have played such an important part in bringing this book to life? More importantly, how do I list everyone without leaving someone out?!

You know who you are and how vitally important you are in my life. From elementary, high school, and college partners in crime (smile), to influencers in my early professional years; lifelong friends, sounding boards, and my life partner. Extra appreciation and gratitude to everyone who graciously gave me draft edit and note input. You're all, every one of you, reflected in these pages. Thank you for your insights, lessons, and most of all – your love and acceptance.

Special shoutouts to Rones, for loving me enough to put the words on the page; Thom, for taking me (okay, dragging me) along on our "adventures"; Dixson, for being; Judith Ann, for loving me for more than 30 years; Linda, for being my very own personal therapist since high school; Sharon, for sharing the joys of education with me; Diva, for making such beautiful music for me to dance to; Arnold-Massey, for helping me finish that dissertation research; Allison, for sharing Rhys with me; Sissy, for loving my son; Grandchildren, for making me a "Gram;" Katherine, Myko and Alex, for letting me be your personal version of "Auntie Mame;" and to Mommy, for giving me life.

FOREWORD

joyce has superbly done it again! In her latest book, she compiles funny anecdotes and quotes and weaves them in a compelling way, breathing life into the weighty subject of transformational leadership. *What Am I Supposed to Say?* is a must read for leaders in all walks of life who are not only looking to execute on tactics, but also transform their organization.

I first met joyce through her work as an executive coach while working in Pensacola, Florida. Quite candidly, I didn't realize I needed coaching at the time. (laugh!) I remember during one of my early coaching sessions with her, I'd basically shown up and done a full verbal dump of all the craziness of my world – operational cost cutting, outside consultants, new boss, department reorganization, etc. One of the first things I noticed was how great a listener she is. Her ability to distill information into a simple problem statement and ask for feedback inspired me to think more deeply about my own management and leadership style. During those coaching sessions, joyce would always share a quote and overarching theme that would be perfect for the moment. Those themes often come to mind and serve as guiding principles as I continue to develop as a leader. She has an uncanny knack of drawing insights about leadership that have parallels to your favorite movie scenes, author, or music.

Oh, so how did my verbal vomit session end up? joyce asked me a simple question. "How do you go about time management?" As it turns out, I had a lot of work to do in that area! I am so appreciative of joyce's coaching and advice as I still use her question methodology regarding time management today. (Especially now with the abundance of virtual meetings.) Does it require a meeting? Does it have to be done now? Do I need to be in the meeting? Who should be in the meeting?

What makes joyce's advice so impactful is that she has lived it through her various roles in industry and academia. She freely shares her successes and failures and what she has learned from each one. joyce has 'walked the walk' and now you get the chance to learn from her insights in *What am I Supposed to Say?* and find your own voice in becoming a transformational leader.

Foster Ware
Customer Experience Manager
Alabama Power
October 2020

Foster previously served on the board of Trustees at Tuskegee University. He is a graduate of the Kellogg School of Management at Northwestern University and lives in Birmingham, AL with his wife Linda and their four children.

INTRODUCTION

"… there is no new thing under the sun," (Book of Ecclesiastes) is an appropriate way to begin this book on leadership. My previous book, *Why Are They Following Me?* (Best Gurl, 2017) focused on lessons I learned during my 40+ years as a leader and how to encourage and lead those who chose to follow me. *What Am I Supposed to Say?* takes the words of those who came before me, my own, and those of people I admire and looks at them through the lens of transformative leadership as applied to businesses, communities, families, classrooms … life.

Much has been researched and written about Transformational Leadership and the changes that resulted since James Downton coined the phrase in 1973. Many have followed in his footsteps, testing the theory and refining his methods since then. As my crafting buddy and professional colleague, Allison Fitzpatrick says, "Much of management and leadership involves influencing those who are supposed to follow you. How can you be a leader if no one wants to be behind you? You need to exhibit confidence and competence and your team needs to trust you. This depends on how you make your team feel." It requires leaders to be consistent in expectations and hold themselves to an even higher standard than what is expected of followers. Not seeing themselves as heroes riding in to save the day, or having all the answers. Knowing that their followers are "affected by and care about the decisions" they make (Steven B. Sample). Taking action and incorporating behaviors that bring about transformation in the lives of others. All with the goal of encouraging followers to go beyond their own interests and seek the best for an organization, family, school, or community.

While actions are vital, words can be just as important. A huge part of leading is figuring out how, when, and what to say ... or not say, so that transformation can take place. I've often said that sometimes silence is the best answer, except when it's not! No matter who is following you ... children, partner, employees, or volunteers; there are always going to be times when they come to you for guidance, encouragement, reinforcement, or direction. Knowing what to say can be challenging. Over the years, I've occasionally seen or heard a phrase, expression, or response that resonated within me. Some were from famous people, others I read in books or heard in movies or TV, and still more were heard during conversations or seminars. I've tucked them all away in my brain or written them down and inevitably, I've found myself digging one of them out for myself or for someone else. Wherever I know who said or wrote the quotation, it's been cited for you. Lots of times I don't even remember where I read or heard it! But it really doesn't matter, if I can figure out what to say at the right time. Some of those same people have come back to ask me what I'd said to them ... sometimes I remember ... sometimes I don't!

The common thread is usually related to change ... transformation; dealing with it, preparing for it, or recovering from it. Your job is to help people who are depending on and following you navigate their way through as successfully as possible. They want to know that you are worth following; part of that requires you to know or be able to figure out what to say, or what not to say, or having an example to share in that moment when they feel angry, sad, or afraid of what is currently going on or looming ahead. Another part is you knowing how to get the performance and commitment that the community, organization, school, or family needs if it is going to be successful.

I decided to collect the words that have shaped and inspired me, add my thoughts to some of them, and put them in this rather unconventional guide to leadership. Even though it's really a book to remind me, I'm going to share it with you and hope that it's helpful. Like my first book, *Why Are They Following Me?* this one isn't a "how-to," rather, it's a "whom to." Focusing on the essence of leadership, not the 5-easy steps. Sometimes, in *What Am I Supposed to Say?* I reflect upon the quotation and share leadership lessons I've learned as a result of seeing the difference it's made when incorporated into my life or how it impacted the lives of others. Other times, I just include the quotation, without any reflection of my own; either because it is universally understood or to simply let you reflect on the possible application for your own life. Use this guide for yourself … or for anyone who sometimes struggles with what to say that will transform or inspire. I've found each phrase or quote to be transformative for me, and hope you will too!

WHAT IS IT ABOUT RELATIONSHIPS?

getting along and interacting with others

We teach people how to treat us by the way we respond to their treatment, so if you don't like the way you're treated, don't blame the other person.

There is a lot of talk in the world today about people deserving respect and from whom they want it. Let's flip that script for just a minute. Every day, in every single interaction you have with others, you teach people how to treat you when you respond. If your children and partners leave dirty clothes all over and you go in, pick them up, and wash them anyway … you've taught them it's okay to leave dirty clothes lying around because you'll wash them anyway. Don't wash anything that isn't in the laundry basket/room for a week, two weeks, and they'll change the behavior faster than they ever will when you fuss at them while you're picking up the clothes! What if a follower doesn't complete the project or report in a way that gives you all the information you need? You spend hours "filling in the blanks" instead of giving the report back to him, explaining what is missing and when you want another revision turned in … yep, you've taught him to do a half-baked job. How about when the sales person ignores you while talking on the phone rather than checking you out and receiving your payment? You stand there huffing, rolling your eyes, and muttering until she finishes …. Walk away, leave the purchase and immediately contact (or find) the manager/owner to let him or her know that you will not return and that you are going to tell everyone you know. Be clear, don't be emotional, use the DESC model from *Why Are They Following Me?* (Describe the behavior. Express how it affects you and others. State what you want. Convey the consequence of not complying.)

Teach them, and train them. Don't let one item or issue slip by. Respond the first time and every time … and implement the consequences as promised. Then, you can stop complaining about how someone is treating you. Because, "In the end, you know what? I'm the only one responsible for what I chose to do," Gregory Maguire.

The Golden Rule is, "Do unto others as you would have others do unto you."
The Platinum Rule is, "Do unto others as they want to be done unto," so
take the time to find out what the other person wants.

It's easy to give a follower, colleague, or friend the things you like and hope, or assume, she likes the same things … except when she doesn't. If she never, ever eats chicken and you invite her to share your lunch of … chicken salad because you made way too much …. If she always sits apart from everyone else in the break room, reading and you go over, plop down to start talking because you want to get to know her …. If she has an ill child and is torn between being at work or being at the hospital and you either send her to a conference so she has a "break" or give her a pay bonus rather than giving her paid time off …. If she likes jelly beans and you give her chocolate …. Well, you get the picture!

Say what you mean and mean what you say!
Enough said.

Are you crazy? How are you crazy? Can I tell you about my crazy?

This is another of my favorites … too bad I don't remember where I heard it. Probably in my car because the piece of notepaper it's written on is from one of the notepads I keep in Penelope (my Prius). I heard it on the radio, NPR most likely, and it just resonated. I think we all ask those questions of each other on a daily basis. We're all basically some version of "crazy" and knowing that, it means we are sane. Gerald Goodman, PhD, an emeritus professor of psychology at UCLA says, "Believing that you are going crazy is a good clue that you are sane." In many ways, it's how we ask for reassurance from those around us. "Talk me down," is a frequently used expression when we are anxious or worried about some incident or action. The important thing for you to remember is that we all have our own version of crazy and it's uniquely our own. Find out what it is for the person who needs you, learn to recognize when it rears its head, and be able to reassure him that he isn't crazy, just feeling anxious or misunderstood. Then work with him to resolve the trigger. Be sure you have someone who can talk you down from your own crazy as well!

Being deeply loved by someone gives you strength, while loving someone deeply gives you courage, Lao Tzu.

It's an awful feeling to love someone so much that you hate them for leaving you, even before they're gone, Charlotte, in *Mr. Church.*

This was an amazing film about a young girl named Charlotte and her mother who were cared for by a male housekeeper, Mr. Church, throughout her mother's illness and death. Although he remained aloof and private, Charlotte and Mr. Church came to respect and eventually love each other. As is often the case in relationships, words were unspoken, assumptions were made and reformed, and in the end ... all that mattered was the deep love and respect they had for each other and the changes they made on each other's lives. Makes me think about who my relationships impact and how ....

The measure of love is what it unselfishly gives.

How much of my giving is motivated by a desire to receive, versus the desire to see someone benefit from my giving?

In *Why Are They Following Me?* I wrote about the importance of a leader loving his followers. I still believe in the importance of that. When you love those who follow you, whether professionally or personally, you seek their best; what is good for them. You identify a course for an employee who shared that he would like to learn to code so that he could do more on the company website. You pair another employee with a colleague of yours as a mentor because she told you about the kind of position she would like to have one day. You send your nephew tickets to a concert for his favorite band. You give what has meaning and value to the receiver, not you necessarily; unless you like your nephew's favorite band and decide to go with him! Learning how to give, when to give, and to whom is fundamental to transformative leadership.

The whole point of good manners is to prevent bumps in the road, or to smooth them over if they can't be avoided, Philip Galanes.

Good manners are not for the sake of "rules" or "judgment," but to have an environment where people can relax and enjoy each other's company. I love this quote!

Too often, people see good manners or etiquette as a list of things to do in order to show that you have class or polish. That's so far from reality it isn't funny … at least to me. Good manners help make others comfortable in your presence, not make them feel inadequate or inept. Good manners mean greeting a newcomer with a smile, fist bump or hug, depending on the circumstances, and introducing her to at least one other person in the group with whom she has something in common so that she doesn't feel left out in a room full of people who know each other. Good manners mean not creating your own little garbage pile around your place at a table that others have to look at or clean up. Good manners mean walking over and introducing yourself to the guy standing alone. Good manners mean signaling the waiter when someone spills, giving your seat to an elderly gentleman who is carrying multiple bags of groceries on the train or bus, or just chewing with your mouth closed so no one has to watch you masticate your food … ugh! Good manners mean saying "Please" "Thank you" and "You're welcome" often and to everyone, regardless of their status. Good manners make people feel good when you're around.

I grew up watching the president of a Fortune 500 company chatting with a teacher's aide because they were introduced to each other on the basis of sharing a common interest. There were no social stations at events. No one was introduced by title or rank, but by name and interest or passion. Good manners were used to provide an opportunity for people to interact with strangers. It was a wonderful example of what a great hostess does. Don't just invite people and leave them on their own … they'll just gravitate to others whom they already know. That drives me batty! Make the effort to forge connections between people. After all, you invited them to the party, so make sure they don't hit a speed bump.

I've learned that people will forget what you said, people will forget what you did, but people will never forget how you made them feel, Maya Angelou.

It's hard to miss someone who's always around.

Familiarity breeds contempt, or so says the proverb. Thom and I laugh about how we always knew when one of us was ready for him to get on a plane (or in the car) and head back to LA or for me to head back home if I was out there. It didn't have anything to do with whether or not we loved and liked each other. It had to do with allowing our relationship, and each other, to grow. Being apart for a period of time allowed us time to experience, reflect, fail, struggle, and develop. Coming back together gave us adventures to share, issues to puzzle out together, a vision to seek; and a renewed appreciation for the relationship. The same is true for those who are following you. Give them some space … and don't be a pest!

When people try to show you who they really are, believe them the first time … don't make them keep having to show you, Maya Angelou.

I'm not talking about the one-off bad day or mistake. I'm talking about always interrupting others … arrogant; not cleaning up their own messes …

inconsiderate; gossiping … disloyal; spreading untruths … not trustworthy. I'm talking about standard mode of operation. She's always late for everything and just laughs it off when you protest. He never returns your phone call or acknowledges your email. She always tells the most embarrassing stories about you to people you've just met. He consistently demeans his coworkers, in a group, in front of them. She never makes all of the corrections you ask for on reports or documents.

You get the idea. These behaviors are the "fall back" and the norm. They don't, won't, and aren't going to change. When you really see him, believe him. He is showing you who he is. The decision is yours. Is this someone you want in your life? As a follower? As a leader? If you're okay with the behaviors, fine, no problem. However, if you're not, then you have a decision to make. You've told him over and over how you feel about it; you've asked her to stop. Are you going to allow it to continue? You are the only one who can make that decision. You won't change him and you won't make her stop, so change your own behavior instead.

Remember that you're not powerless. When you're supposed to meet outside the restaurant at 5:00 and it's 5:10, go inside to be seated and order your meal. When she arrives, chat and when you're finished with your meal, explain why you're leaving and ask for what you want in the future (DESC), pay the check for your meal, and leave. Stop calling or sending email to him if he is a friend, have a disciplinary meeting and document it if he is an employee. Stop going places with her and if it cannot be avoided, when she launches into a story, interrupt her and change the subject to a topic the group can discuss, and keep doing it every time. You get the idea. Change your behavior when you are around these people, or sever the relationship. Don't make them keep showing you who they are. If you won't address it, then stop complaining.

That which is said, cannot be unsaid ... or forgotten, Danish Proverb.

Wow, just wow. This is such a powerful statement, one that, too often, we don't think about. You may regret the words the instant they leave your mouth. It's too late. Those words can never be unheard. Say them in your head or alone in the car, if you must. But once you say them **to** someone, you can never, ever, ever take them back.

No matter what I feel in the moment, as soon as the words leave my mouth they are always spoken and I can never rewind the clock to take them back. Hurtful, angry, cruel words live forever ... just as loving, kind, and generous ones do. I have the choice about what comes out of my mouth. And let's be honest, if it's someone I know well, I know exactly what to say and how to say it to inflict the most damage.

How often have you said something in anger, hurt, or frustration only to wish, five minutes, or five seconds later, that you hadn't? Watching the reaction of the other person. Seeing the pain in her eyes can be almost as devastating for you as it is for her hearing your words. How much better would it be if you taught yourself to just walk away until you can express what you need or feel in a way that isn't harmful to the listener? We can lose a lifetime of trust and respect with just a few words ... and never get them back again.

Never underestimate the power or the impact of "like."

Like is sometimes even more powerful and lasting than love.

I love everyone who has ever followed or will ever follow me. I will push him to go beyond what he thinks he can achieve. I will stop her from using her power to intimidate or dominate others. Because of that decision to love. Not the emotional hearts and flowers; rather, a love that seeks the highest and best in others. So yes, I love my followers ... I haven't liked all of them and all of them haven't liked me.

The ones I liked (or vice versa) have remained part of my life; long after our official relationship ended. They still seek my input, and I theirs. The ones I simply loved, moved on.

Why can't a woman be like me?

Those who have seen the musical, *My Fair Lady* (based on the play, *Pygmalion* by George Bernard Shaw) will recognize the words sung by Professor Henry Higgins' character.

> *Why can't a woman be more like a man?*
> *Men are so honest, so thoroughly square;*
> *Eternally noble, historically fair.*
> *Who, when you win, will always give your back a pat.*
> *Why can't a woman be like that?*

Higgins is baffled by the fact that Eliza, the woman he has taken in and to whom he has taught proper speech, dress, and decorum, has run off heartbroken because he praised himself for her accomplishments and (from her perspective), never praised or recognized the effort she contributed. Sound familiar?

Have you ever been in a situation where you poured everything you had into reaching the goal that had been set for you or your tribe (family, coworkers, friends)? Doing things that you thought you couldn't because of your belief in the goal and the leader who set the bar? Only to reach glorious accomplishment and hear her talking with others, taking the credit when describing what "she" did. How did you feel? What was your initial reaction or response? One of the keys to successful leadership is to take the blame and give the credit … all the time, every time. Nothing is accomplished in a silo and there is no "I" in the word "Team." Remember that when those who have put their trust in you worked to accomplish the task(s) and recognize their contributions; don't take the credit. It will go a long way toward maintaining their trust and commitment.

We must learn to love ourselves before we can love someone else.

Normal people worry me, bumper sticker on my car, Penelope.

You know the ones. They must do, be, or have whatever "everyone else" does, is, or possesses. They want to fit in, blend in, not be isolated or thought to be different. So, they contort and distort themselves into what they see as normal, leaving behind the uniqueness they are capable of manifesting.

She never rises to the top because she is conforming to the style of her CEO. Using his power to give her validity. Or using her charm to attract followers rather than her intellect and ability to envision possibilities. Being "normal." Fitting in. Not making waves. Ultimately, losing herself.

As you can imagine, "There is no box," is my advice. Anyone can be normal. Not everyone has the resilience and courage to be herself!

Do you suppose there are wounds, which go so deep, the healing of them hurts as much as the wounding? Percy, in *The Spitfire Grill.*

Yes! Resoundingly Yes!!

There are some wounds people carry that go all the way to their core. Just as the creation of them took time, pain, and (sometimes) intentionality, so must the healing. As a leader, you can help uncover the wound, often cutting the area open again. Expose it to light. Provide opportunities for cleaning. Allow faltering and feelings of defeat while offering the water of wisdom to flush out any toxins and a cleanly bandaged surface to practice and heal.

It takes time, pain, and intentionality; and as the one they follow, you owe them nothing less.

I'd always secretly believed that a love as fierce and true as mine would be rewarded in the end, and now I was being forced to accept the bitter truth, Alma Katsu.

Sometimes, no matter how much you love a follower, her behavior ultimately causes harm to the rest of a team. She loves and seeks her own ambitions more than the ambitions of the whole. When that time comes, you must let her go.

At one point in my career, I hired a young woman with limited experience and a ton of potential. After almost a year, I thought she could be my successor. (You usually don't get promoted until you've groomed or identified your successor – even if nobody tells you that.) We began adding responsibilities and expanding the scope of her role. She flourished. Until she didn't.

It was a small thing, really. A change of position and a change of location. The opportunity for her to expand her knowledge, demonstrate some leadership, and interact with others at similar and different positional levels. She failed miserably. Rather than seeing the opportunity for what it was, being groomed to succeed me, she felt that she had been cast aside and began listening to the occasional grumblings and complaining until eventually, she was adding to and embellishing the grumbling and she began complaining the loudest. Needless to say, the situation ended very badly for many people, including me, because of her actions.

No, she ultimately didn't ever get what she wanted. She did get what she deserved!

Truth may be vital, but without love it is unbearable, Pope Francis (Jorge Mario Bergoglio).

We often talk about speaking the truth to others. Most of the time, the sentiment is from a self-righteous or "I'm right, you're wrong" perspective. And how does that work for you? (laughing) Thought so. Whenever we don't speak the truth in love, we just won't be heard. Period.

I'm not upset that you lied to me, I'm upset that from now on I can't believe you, Friedrich Nietzsche.

Okay, confession time. I really do love the works of Nietzsche. Sorry. Not Sorry. He had a way of cutting through all the external fluff and stripping us to our elemental selves. Raw, feeling, thinking, searching humans bumping into each other on a planet that is at once too vast and too small. If she really thinks about it, she isn't upset that her friend lied … people tell lies, large and usually small, all the time. The problem comes when she discovers one of those lies, usually the small one, and then realizes that she questions everything else he says. That makes her angry because she never had to think about what he told her before and now she has to spend extra energy in their relationship, wondering if this thing or that is in fact true when she used to just be able to enjoy her relationship with him. So, yes finding out that someone lied, at the core, makes you upset with yourself and the second-guessing you do from that point forward. Make sure truth always comes from you. Even when … especially when, it's hard.

Relationships are like a virus, and the people involved, separately, are the host cells. The key is to find a relationship, a virus, that encourages you to be stronger, a better person, but also be able to show weakness without fear of exploitation – a relationship that challenges you, but also makes you happy and lifts you up, Penny Reid.

I stumbled across this practically perfect statement about relationships. What a great description! Just like some viruses will cause fatal diseases, some relationships are likewise "fatal" to our self-esteem, our growth, our ability to contribute to others and society. Other viruses are like the oncolytic ones being studied for their ability to fight and even destroy cancer cells without harming other cells.

What "viruses" exist in your relationships? Are they causing harm and need to be removed? Are they strengthening and challenging you to be better than you are? How can you know? Simple, if something makes you physically ill, you avoid it … same as with people. Don't allow the influence of unhealthy virus people in your life. Whether at work, home, or play. Evaluate the benefits versus the adverse effects of your relationships, then take steps to build your immune system. Spend as much time as possible with people who challenge your thinking and develop your skills. Don't continue to accept being treated lousy. Remove those people (or yourself) from the relationship.

We are afraid to care too much, for fear that the other person does not care at all, Eleanor Roosevelt.

Sometimes we, especially those who love deeply and more unconditionally, tend to pull back the reins on how much and to whom we give our love. The problem is, when we do that, we risk missing out on relationships that are solid, true, and lasting. We avoid taking that "next step," when we should leap; we lose out on a friendship, mentor, protégé, or intimate relationship because we are afraid. We miss opportunities to benefit from the talents and contributions of someone else; and perhaps most important, to grow our thinking and expand our appreciation of those whose perspective is different from our own. When we hold back because we are afraid to care we limit our growth. Fear causes us to build a wall between ourselves and the very ones who could enrich our lives.

Let's clear one thing up: Introverts do not hate small talk because we dislike people. We hate small talk because we hate the barrier it creates between people, Laurie Helgoe.

The first time I read this, I had to stop and read it again. Then, again. One more time with a smile and head nod. There was such a resonance within me that I just stopped reading. Finally, someone translated my intent when I say, "I don't like people."

May I say, without shame, guilt, or remorse – that I despise small talk? I usually get silent; not smile, not make eye contact while the talker, or talkers, chatter on. I also am often told afterward what a good listener I am; not too difficult when you have no idea what to say and no interest in figuring it out. When, on the rare occasion, I ask, "How are you?" I mean it and want to know how you *really* are. On the even more rare occasions that I answer, "How are you?" questions, my answer is lengthy and deeply felt. Because ... I despise small talk. I also have an internal radar signal telling me when it matters how I answer, so when I sense that it doesn't matter or isn't really being listened to, I don't answer. Guess what?! The other person almost never notices (laughing).

Decades ago, for one month, I conducted an experiment. Everywhere I went, whenever I was asked, "How are you?" I answered the way I was really feeling. "Sad today; Great; Doing okay; Hungry; Tired ..." whatever I was, that's how I answered – no matter who it was or where I was. Here is what I found out. Almost every person, almost every time, responded, "That's good," or some variation of that. They didn't even hear my honest response. A few would blink once or twice in surprise, then move on to more small talk. That's when I stopped responding. Now, I just say, "Hi" or "Hello," in response to, "How are you?" or whatever variation is used.

Is that awful of me? Probably. Does it bother me? Not really, and here's why: the people in my life; loved ones, friends, clients, and colleagues who really do want to know, ask, and if necessary, ask again because they can see or sense that something's going on. The ones who are closest to me don't waste time and just ask, "What's wrong?" They get an answer, a heartfelt answer. I don't want nicety barriers between me and the people I care about. They are too important to me, even if I'm not as important to them. When I see or talk to my inner circle, I don't want to waste our time together on small talk because I can't stand the barrier it creates between us. Transformative leaders usually don't either.

It's good to care about what others think, but only when those other people matter, Penny Reid.

Mommy and I were on one of our Saturday, North Michigan Avenue adventures. Shopping, browsing, eating, and chatting … I was only about eight or nine, so we still liked each other. As we wandered through Field's, someone called her name and we stopped to see one of the most hateful, and mean-to-children, new teachers at Mommy's school approaching. To be fair, the children all knew it. The administrators and other teachers hadn't figured it out yet. Mommy pulled me to a stop as the woman reached us because yep, my feet were still walking; "Joyce, you remember 'Miss Harrison', don't you?" she asked me. Silence. "Joyce, say hello to Miss Harrison." Silence. "Joyce," short, clipped and with that narrow – eyed glare that was so familiar. Silence. "Joyce. Karen. Gillie. Say. Hello. To. Miss. Harrison." Now with the dragon-whisper voice. My brain was thinking, calculating, then it came, "But you told me never speak to strangers, Mommy." Steam. Out of her ears. Meanwhile, Miss Harrison did her snooty-nasty laugh and reached out to touch me. I immediately stepped behind Mommy, which made Mommy pause and look at me.

After some small talk chatter, Miss Harrison walked away and Mommy led me over to some chairs. Mommy asked me, "Why don't you like Miss Harrison, Joyce?" I looked to make sure she really wanted to know, then told her, "Because she doesn't like children," I answered honestly. Surprised expression. Then, "Tell me why you think that," Mommy said. "Because," I began, "she pinches us when we're not in a straight line, even though she isn't our teacher. She pulls the girls' hair if it's longer than hers. She won't let you go to the restroom if you need to go ...." "Joyce," Mommy interrupted me, "how could you possibly know all of this? You're not in her class." "Because she's pinched me and pulled my hair and we all talk about it at recess. She doesn't like us and she is mean to the children." Mommy didn't ask anything else, she just hugged me, then said, "Thank you, Joyce," took my hand, and we resumed our adventure.

Here is the lesson for any parent, teacher, or administrator ... anyone who leads others. When someone who looks to you for protection, guidance, and leadership tells you that someone with more power than she has doesn't like or is mean to her, believe her; unless she is a known chronic liar. She is telling you because she believes you care and what you think matters to her. If Mommy had fussed at me about not speaking or for telling the truth, that would have given me a message about not being as important to her as Miss Harrison was. She didn't. She cared about what I thought, listened, heard me, and did her own research.

None of the children and almost all the teachers were surprised a few months later when Miss Harrison was transferred out of our school. Every child in her class and a whole lot of the rest of us on that floor had a recess celebration that Monday. Mommy never discussed it with me and never had to tell me not to discuss it at school ... she wasn't "Mommy" there (smile). Decades later, we were talking about our careers and I asked her about Miss

Harrison. "She had been transferred twice before for similar things," Mommy told me. "So, you didn't just send her to another school, right?" I asked with a grin. "No," Mommy said. "After talking with other children, then observing myself, she and I had a conversation about what was going on and what her options were. While researching her, I learned that she was good at and enjoyed curriculum development much more than teaching children. I called your Uncle 'Morgan' in Central Office and he was able to transfer her there." Mommy looked at me, smiled, and smoothed her hand down the side of my face. "Thank you for knowing that you could tell me," she said. "Thank *you* for letting me know that the reason for my behavior mattered," I smiled back at her.

WORK, WORK, WORK!

work-life balance, work ethics, productivity

Don't wallow in the grass.

I wrote about the need for leaders to fly at 20,000 or 40,000 feet to be able to see where they're going and the obstacles in the way in *Why Are They Following Me?*. Just as important, leaders cannot and should not get in the grass of day-to-day minutiae operations. Perhaps that's why the people who have subject matter/content expertise often have the most difficulty leading the same kind of organizations or teams. The temptation to "just do it herself" is often too great. Before she knows it, she has taken over laying out the newsletter, writing the proposal, or doing the presentation slides for the sales team. What a waste, and what an insult to the people she expects to follow her.

How can they follow when she isn't leading anywhere? How can they stretch and gain new skills when she takes over as soon as they make a mistake? How can they avoid rocks, hills, and bumps in the road if she only sees them at the same time they do? She's wallowing. It doesn't help any of them. Not her, because she isn't growing and developing new skills; not her followers because they aren't either. Stay out of the grass, I tell my Executive Coaching clients. If she stays out of the grass, she'll have time to strategically plan, develop new product or service ideas, or build critical alliances with new partners; all of which move her organization or team forward! Moving forward is vital for the well-being of herself and her followers … and you have to stay out of the grass!

Eat when you're hungry … Sleep when you're tired.

Sounds like common sense, right?! But how many people actually do it? So many either eat lunch at a certain time, or have employers who schedule lunchtime for them, never considering whether they're hungry or not. We set a time to go to bed, then lie there with racing brain, tossing and turning because we aren't sleepy. Even worse, we don't eat when we are hungry because it isn't "dinner time" yet; and we stay up yawning through that movie/TV show.

Transformative leaders who revolutionize, reform, and alter their landscape, are aware of the need to create a space where followers can eat when they're hungry and sleep when they're tired … literally and figuratively.

Create an environment that lets everyone break free from the automated regimen and express all their creativity and innovation. Stop saying, "can't" or "but" and start saying "what if," "how could," or "yes, and …" to meet the challenges that come. Ask followers what they need from you to be successful at the job/goal/project you've given them, and figure out how to provide what they need. When you do, if you do, you'll discover that they are more productive and innovative because they can sleep when they're tired and that they have more energy because they can eat when they're hungry. They benefit, you benefit, and the organization thrives.

You can have it all; just not at the same time, Ruth Bader Ginsberg, by attribution.

Frequently, when I'm speaking to a group, I'll say this especially when it's a group of women. Society has placed an expectation on women to "do it all" that isn't placed on men. She must always look great (well-dressed, hair, nails, makeup), be intelligent **and** smart, able to reason and learn, keep a perfect and orderly household (clean, laundry, decorate, cook, entertain, shop); take care of all gifts and special occasions, plan and orchestrate perfect travel and vacations, have high achieving and well-mannered children, achieve the highest levels in her profession, and be the perfect wife/partner (supportive, sacrificing, selfless). When you put it that way, of course it's impossible! It's still the expectation.

Conflict between a child's school event and a business trip? Scheduling overlap with significant other? Washing machine repair at the same time as carpool turn? Birthday party on the same day as a report is due? Why doesn't the school alternate between parents when a child needs to be picked up from school? (Thanks, RBG.) You get the picture. No matter the choice, something or someone misses out and she is too often told, or tells herself, that she doesn't have the right priorities, is a poor planner, is selfish, or only cares about herself. Granted, men can be on the receiving end as well. Yet societally, too often there is an unspoken expectation for him to choose his professional life and for her to choose her personal life. When that doesn't happen, the accusations and emotional punishment begins … for both. It's not fair, for either; and it's reality for both. So, I repeat; you can have it all, just not at the same time (RBG). Make choices about what is realistic and what is not. Decide for yourself what takes priority and when; don't let society's expectations dictate your priorities. Be true to what brings satisfaction and fulfillment even if that means waiting longer for satisfaction in another area of your life. Most of all, accept responsibility for your choices and don't try to impose your choice or priority on someone else.

Nothing defeats high quality like low prices.

When you pay low wages to employees. When you don't treat employees with respect. That's exactly what your customers or clients receive … low quality and no respect from your employees!

Everything takes longer than you think. There are three ways to complete any task: fast, cheap, and best; in any given situation you are likely to only achieve two of the three: fast and cheap, and not the best; fast and the best, not cheap; cheap and the best, not fast, Jim Jarmusch.

If you think I'm kidding, just start a renovation on your home or workplace. When the contractor tells you three months and you find yourself still waiting for completion at the five-month mark, then you'll become a believer!

So, when you assign a project, think about the cost if you want it done fast and best, because you'll have to pay by other things not getting done. Or, allow more time if you can't eliminate everything else and you'll get it done cheap and best, and not fast. If you plan for a fast turnaround without eliminating other responsibilities, then you'll have to plan on redoing and fixing what you ultimately receive because it will be fast and cheap, and not the best.

We can't expect followers to invent time or do everything, including a new complicated project, and have it perfect. Not. Going. To. Happen. I don't care how much you want it to. Your best option is to plan backward from whenever it's due and then add more time to make sure you get the best results on time.

Leaderless people wander aimlessly through life or careers, never knowing what purpose they serve.

Leadership isn't about telling others what to do. It's about harnessing the collective energy and ability of others and using it to guide everyone toward achieving a goal. Making sure he knows how the role he plays is essential to goal achievement. Focusing on progress and growth to ensure that he grows and develops into what and who he needs to be.

Before all negotiations, determine who has the most to gain and who has the most to give. and *Everything is a negotiation.*

I learned this first with my son and it was reinforced by Thom. It is so, so right! The grade on a class assignment, negotiation. The price of a service being provided, negotiation. Establishing a new relationship, negotiation. Finding a solution to a tricky challenge, negotiation. Deciding which route to take to a destination or getting a raise … yep! Negotiation!! What we often fail to realize is that just about everything is a negotiation! Especially in a relationship – not just in business; with children, partners, parents, fiancées, and friends.

Find the common ground or goal first and work from there. Don't start where you are oppositional; she will just dig in and so will you. "Begin with the end in mind," Covey wrote in his *7 Habits*. He was right. The end is a solution that benefits everyone, not just the one with power. As you work toward that solution, listen; don't just wait for your turn. Reflect on her position and needs. Share your own. Don't set up boundaries or walls that have no real meaning or value. Clearly ask for what you need, not necessarily all that you want or would like to have. Push toward an option that meets her needs **and** yours. Be creative. Do what's never been done. Try something different! Negotiate for her benefit … and yours.

When he was two-years old, I told my son Dixson to pick up his toys and go start getting ready for bed. With an adorable face and dimpled smile, he looked at me and said, "Mommy, can we negotiate?" Okay, confession time; I melted … then I internally laughed! "No, bedtime is not negotiable," I replied. "Get moving," I said, still trying to keep a straight face. "Okay Mommy," he grumbled, "I still think we should negotiate this." He grabbed the rope on the laundry basket I'd rigged for him to be able to pick up his toys and drag them to his room. Shaking his head in disgust, he muttered, "What good is negotiate if I don't get to do it?" Good point!

If everything is a negotiation and you know who has the most to gain and give, it does absolutely no good if you don't at least make the effort to try. Otherwise, all you get is what the other person wants to give you … and it may not be what you want, or need.

I could get a lot more done if these people would stop calling me! Customer Service Representative.

I was conducting a Customer Service workshop for a municipal utility client and we were discussing how to be more efficient when one of the Reps made this comment.

To put the situation in context, one of the reasons the client wanted the workshop was that the customer satisfaction survey we conducted for them indicated that the Customer Service Representatives had become "less welcoming and helpful" and "more abrupt and curt" during the last 12-months. We were discussing reasons for the change in behavior. After her comment, there was immediate reaction that included head nods, mutters of, "Yep," "Sure could," and "She's right." Then, there was a pause. A subtle shift in the room took place as everyone began to look at me. Eyes became sheepish and many immediately broke eye contact. Right … their job was to answer the phone and talk with customers! Our focus should be on ways to streamline the follow-up paperwork process, not get rid of or reduce the number of callers. That's what we focused on for the rest of the workshop. By the end of the day, they had successfully reworked the customer follow-up reporting and drastically reduced the amount of time it took, plus eliminated duplication of efforts and redundancies. Listening to what people complain about sometimes gives insight into what they need from you for them to be successful.

When you manage people, figure out what your employees need from you in order for them to be their most successful selves. Some folks need praise, some folks need criticism, some folks need structure. Some folks just need small talk, knowing you care, and that's it. It'll be different for each person. Basically, when you're a leader, it's impossible to treat everyone the same. Each person needs something different from you – as their leader – in order to succeed. Being in charge means figuring out what that thing is for each individual, and then giving it to them, Penny Reid.

I spent an entire section in *Why Are They Following Me?* focusing on the people who follow leaders and ways to give our followers what they need to be successful. I won't repeat all of that here! Instead, let's look at how we can lead others for transformation by figuring out who needs what from you.

Getting to know who your followers are at a behavioral and characteristic level is good for business. Good for students. Good for the bottom line. Good for customers or clients. Most of all, it's good for you as a transformative leader because it allows you to bring about change in the organization and growth in the people who are following you.

If he is direct, big-picture-oriented and structured, then he probably needs for you to get to the bottom line. Tell him the expected outcome, who needs to be involved in the process, give him the time frame and level of detail you require and the resources he has available to him. He doesn't need, or usually want, recommendations or a team. As much as possible, don't limit his options Especially, don't "hover" as he works on the project. As for his professional development, help him grow by giving him difficult assignments, encouraging him to verbalize reasons for his conclusions and working with him to slow down and take time out to relax more. He will contribute to the organization in ways you couldn't have imagined … and he will grow as a professional as well.

If she is direct, big-picture-oriented and informal or highly interpersonal, then she most often needs you to give her the big picture and vision in a way that makes the project exciting and so that she can involve others. Tell her about people who worked on similar projects and their success or strategies. Don't give her too many details – she wants to figure it out for herself. Do recommend a few people she might want to reach out to or work with. Professionally, help her by working on time management. Schedule updates that she can use to keep herself on track to get the project completed on time. Don't let her get distracted by another project or activity and help her stay focused on the project by requiring her to plan out a timeline for completion. She will reach out to and involve others that you wouldn't have thought of including ... and she will deliver results that are usually new, innovative, and exciting.

For the one who wants facts, options, and structure, allow enough time to explore as many possibilities as you can and don't expect her to work on the project with a team. She wants to know the facts associated with the project, how long before you want a recommendation and access to you while she researches so that all of her questions can be answered; and there will be a lot of them! She will also need you to be patient with all of those questions as she processes your responses and asks even more questions. Help professionally by pointing out her potential and self-worth and give "safe" risk-taking opportunities. She will uncover data and information that no one else will; perhaps even more significant, she will ask the questions that no one would have ever thought to ask, resulting in a better outcome for the entire organization.

Finally, if he is good at resolving the office conflicts and squabbles in a way that leaves everyone feeling good about themselves, if pretty much everyone trusts and confides in him and he doesn't like making hasty decisions, then bring him in on those tricky interpersonal issues or projects. Prickly client or student? He's the one to have with you in the meeting. Disgruntled customer? Ask him to find a resolution that works for the customer and for the business. Make him feel valued and he will always deliver in a way that as many as possible can benefit from or live with. Help him develop tolerance for conflict by placing him in situations that require resolution; he will want to work for it because he can't stand conflict, typically. Give him time limits and deadlines that will help him learn not to procrastinate. The result? You will have your own internal negotiator and conflict resolver ... who becomes more confident and better at what he does.

Diversity is being invited to the party. Inclusion is being asked the kind of music you like. Equity is having the music you like be played. Belonging is being asked to help plan the whole party or at least getting your ideas beforehand about what a fun party would look like, Reggie Shuford.

The best way to find out if you can trust somebody is to trust them, Ernest Hemingway.

When I hire someone, I tell him that my trust is his to lose; not the other way around. I've found that it is faster and more revealing to give trust initially instead of trying to make him "earn" it. I mean, how long do you give? What five things (or fifty) does he have to do for me to check that box? Whereas, if I give trust from the start; completely and without reservation, I know **immediately** when he breaks it.

When you go fishing do you want to use the bait you like or the bait the fish like? Ricardo Soria, by attribution.

This is so, so true! If I need the people who are following me to be willing to go in a new or challenging direction, do I share the vision with them in terms of why it makes sense to me or do I share it in terms of why it makes sense to them? The latter, if I want them to follow me. Chief Soria is a master of this. I've watched him do this as a school administrator and as manager of his son, Reid's, singing and performing career. He can size up the goal, figure out what is needed to achieve it, then give each person on his team a perspective of the vision that specifically motivates him or her. I want to be able to do it half as well as he does someday ....

FAMILIES & FRIENDS

partners, children, and everyone else

We love our sons and raise our daughters! traditional saying.

My son used to wish that was the case with him! Daughters, societally, are expected to pick up after themselves and others; learn how to care for and set up a household; nurture and take care of younger siblings or babysit other children; cook; do laundry; shop … you get the picture. Societally, sons are expected to solve problems, fix things, make decisions, negotiate for what they want, and establish relationships for their advantage and advancement.

What if we also taught our daughters the things we traditionally teach our sons *and* also teach our sons the things we traditionally teach our daughters? They both would have all the skills and talents they need to excel; and they would be "different" from their peers. He would know how to plan a menu, shop for ingredients, prepare and artfully plate the meal as well as problem solve to figure out a substitute if the arugula looks off (hint … baby spinach). She would know how to take apart and replace the cord on the still-good lamp in her room as well as the best placement for adequate lighting. So, that's what I did (laughing). When he could walk, his first lesson was cleaning up after himself. I tied a rope to a small laundry basket and made that easy. Next came bed-making. So what if it was messy, he was only three! Then fixing his breakfast. Lots of spilled milk, bread, and cereal! Fixing a broken toy. Think wobbly truck wheels. At 16, first checking account – and discovering overdraft. Was he different? Yes. Did he hate me for it? Duh … of course! (laughing) Forty years later, is he glad?

He now thanks me on a regular basis because he left home able to completely take care of and make decisions for himself. He could solve problems and stock a kitchen with equal skill. It took a while for him to bounce back from trying to be "normal." Yet here he is working to grow, stretch, and develop fully into an amazing man. So, nope … I loved *and* raised my son and would have done the same thing if he had been a daughter.

When your child turns seventeen: You, "What do you want for dinner?" Her, "I don't know." You (later) "Dinner's ready!" Her, "You never fix what I like! There's never anything I like to eat!" Ginger and Myko Campbell.

Although this was an actual conversation my niece had with her mother, it could be any teen/almost adult in the world. Change the words and it could be any coworker, employer, or employee also! So many times, we don't know what we want, **and** we don't know what we don't want either, until we see it! Think about working with the student you advise at your university. She doesn't know what she wants to major in, so you set up an exploratory schedule for her next semester. One that will allow her to explore the arts, sciences, sociologies, and education fields so that she gets a taste of multiple areas and has a framework for selection. Just a few weeks into the semester, right before drop/add deadlines, she comes into your office and exclaims, "I hate these classes, none of these subjects are right for me. I want to major in business." Taking a deep breath, you pull up the scheduling options, avoid telling her that she never would have known that she wanted to major in business had she not explored the other possibilities, and start changing her schedule!

He'd lived with his mother, with the Wicked Witch of the West (which might be the name of any mother, all mothers) he realized, Gregory Maguire.

I'm laughing too hard to type!! Let me just make this one simple … see "We love our sons and raise our daughters."

To be without friends is a serious form of poverty, Aloysius T. McKeever in *It Happened on 5th Avenue.* and *Don't confuse physical proximity (think coworker or neighbor) with emotional intimacy (think best friend or partner). There are many people with whom you are friendly; few with whom you are actually friends.*

Know the difference!

You don't need many, just a few people with whom you can be your deepest (and share your darkest) self with. The rest are people with whom you're "friendly." They aren't "friends." We use the word friend too often and too loosely. We can't possibly be friends with all the people we lightly award that title to ....

Alex Lickerman wrote, "If one 'friend' needs the support of the other on a consistent basis such that the person depended upon receives no benefit other than the opportunity to support and encourage, while the relationship may be significant and valuable, it can't be said to define a true friendship." I love this insight because it goes beyond our traditional thinking about friendship. He also uses the Japanese word, "kenzoku," which means "family." Lickerman suggests that kenzoku is a "bond between people who've made a similar commitment and who possibly therefore share a similar destiny. It implies the presence of the deepest connection of friendship."

Think about all the people in your life. How many of them go beyond common interest or shared history? Which ones are committed to your happiness and will do whatever they can to ensure it, never expecting you to reciprocate? Which ones have never or will never ask you to do anything that would compromise your core principles? Which ones are always encouraging you and serve as a good influence? When you narrow the field using these criteria ... you've found your friend, your kenzoku. Know and commit to your friends; recognize your friendlies. Treasure your friend and be as loyal and faithful as she is to you!

If you don't receive love from the ones who are meant to love you, you will never stop looking for it, Robert Goolrick.

Most of us know these people. Some of us are this person. When a child doesn't receive what he needs from a significant adult during the formative years (parent, sibling, grandparent) he can spend much of his adult life searching for someone to provide it (spouse, employer, children). Because that basic and fundamental need for love – appreciation, support, unconditionality, inclusion – is a gaping hole.

Are we going to be friends forever? Asked Piglet. Even longer, Pooh answered, A. A. Milne.

There is exactly a handful of women I will be friends with forever. I don't need to name them because they know who they are (smile). I've known them 20-to-40+ years.

No matter when, how, or what I have needed, she steps in; usually all of them. No matter what, when, or how she has needed; I am there for her. We don't talk daily. We don't text or message regularly. Yet somehow, on a day that I'm struggling emotionally or physically, there will be a note or a package in the mail; a voice or text message from her. I often feel inadequate as her friend, having benefitted from the years of her love, support, and mostly her acceptance. She's seen me at my best and at my worst and still loves me anyway … even when I am unlovable. She will be with me forever through our respective common bonds. The bonds that brought us together continue to hold us today. Music. Leadership. Writing. Laughing. Refusing normalcy. Children. Teaching. The list is never ending.

I am grateful to these women. They have saved and transformed me. Hopefully, I have given a measure of that back to them.

There is nothing I would not do for those who are really my friends. I have no notion of loving people by halves; it is not my nature, Jane Austen.

Family cannot be determined by blood. Family is determined by actions. Family is about trust. Family is about acceptance. Family is about love. True family is earned, not born, Sarah Brianne. and *Happiness is having a large, loving, caring, close-knit family in another city,* George Burns.

Growing up, we were fortunate in many ways. One of the most valuable things we were told was that although we were family, it didn't mean we had to like each other because we could choose our friends, and we couldn't choose our family. That means sometimes it's best when you, or they, live somewhere else so that you have some measure of control over their ability to interfere with and influence your life and peacefulness. You can visit when, or if, you want. You can invite or not invite them into your inner circle. When necessary, you can completely shut the door, especially if their presence is toxic for you and for others. Doesn't mean you love them any less … it just means you value your own sanity and peace more!

There was something about the people you grew up around, the ones you'd seen throughout your childhood, the folks you couldn't remember not knowing. Even if the past was a complicated mess, as you aged, you were just glad the [so-and-so's] were still on the planet, J.R. Ward.

I have a few favorite family members I grew up with. Doesn't mean that I love them more than the others who grew up with us; it just means that I like them more.

We have a shared past, all of us. Our memories may be slightly different because of our age or perspective at the time. Yet, when one of us died a few years ago, even though he wasn't one of my favorites, I miss him. As adults, we weren't close, we were too different ... or maybe too much alike; I'm not sure. At the same time, I was still glad that he was here.

The same is true for most people. Everyone has siblings, cousins, almost-relatives we grew up with. The family we have shared experiences and arguments with. We're glad they're around, even if not tied directly into our lives as adults. We know that we can always connect, even if only momentarily, through those experiences. We can laugh (usually) about the childhood squabbles. We have a past. We share history. They transformed us. That history disappears when they do and only lives on in our memories, regardless of how we feel about them as adults.

Those who have no compassion have no wisdom, Benjamin Hoff. and *Compassion is unconditional love applied to the suffering of others*, Mathieu Richard.

Wisdom, being wise, is having experience, retaining the experience as knowledge, and using that knowledge to exercise good judgment in the situations I face. Being confronted with an issue or obstacle, if I am wise, I'm able to draw on my experience in similar situations, remember what I did well or not so well, and make a decision in the current situation that has better results. So, what does that have to do with compassion?

Being compassionate toward others is very different from sympathy or even empathy. My feelings about the situation she finds herself in compel me to take action to alleviate her situation. That's where my wisdom and transformative leadership comes in. Unless I have learned from my own experience, I won't recognize her similar one, feel the need to act because I suffer with her, and know what actions to take that will help relieve her suffering. Wisdom.

One of my (small handful of) friends learned that her mother is in onset dementia and Alzheimer's disease. She was, understandably, devastated. She and her mom are close, they are more than "mother and daughter," they're friends. They spend time with each other doing the activities and crafts they both enjoy; browsing in book and craft stores, trying out new recipes, and going to her children's school events and celebrations. Almost all of that is gone for her now, even though her mom is still here. I sympathize. Because of my own loss, I even empathize. Most important, I have compassion for my friend, which causes me to do whatever I can with and for her. What do I do?

Schedule "get away" breaks for her to come visit. We found a yarn crawl in Asheville, NC, to do together. Carve out hours to just let her talk … and me listen. Research so that I understand the progression and symptoms of the diseases. Share my own feelings and experiences when she asks for them. Whatever it takes. Unconditionally. With love. Through action.

Someone you know is experiencing something similar to your own life experience. They need more than just sympathy or empathy. They need compassion. They need wisdom. The real question is, will you give it to them?

If I care about you, why would I intentionally do something to irritate, upset, or disappoint you?

I'll never forget the day, early in our marriage, I said those words to my husband and partner, Thom Gossom, Jr. He was home from working in Los Angeles (he's an actor) and was upset about something (who knows what it was at this point) I had done … or moved … or changed. I listened to him fussing, while trying not to just fuss right back. When he was finished, I looked at him and said, "I'm sorry. I love you. Why would I intentionally do something to irritate you? So, that means I didn't know it would irritate you when I did it. Now that I know, I won't do it again," and walked out of the room ... because that was about all I could manage without blowing up at that moment (laughing). He got this funny look on his face, like he just realized the truth of my statement and it had never occurred to him before. We often use that with each other when one of us is upset about something the other did. It helps us to remember ... daily, sometimes. It's also helpful to remember with the people you have been selected to lead. They trust you. They believe in you. They're following you. That means they didn't know that whatever it is they did would be the wrong thing to do when they did it ... so give them a break and keep it in perspective!

LOOKING FORWARD; LOOKING BACK

regrets and achievements, dreams and setbacks, holding on and letting go

Never run back to what broke you, Sarah Breedlove (Madam CJ Walker).

If you always do what you've always done, you will always get what you've always gotten. and *Stop doing the things that don't get you what you want.*

Some say that Einstein called it the definition of insanity … I agree (not that anyone asked my opinion). How often in relationships with others as a leader or especially as a follower, do we repeat the same behaviors and get angry, sad, disgusted, or surprised when the results stay the same? If we want something to change, we must change our behavior first; not try to change the situation or the other person. Especially not by continuing to do the same things.

Everything I'm doing gives energy back, it doesn't take it away, Cheryl Jones.

When we think about our daily interactions as fuel for our spirits, rather than detractions from "doing something else," we generate energy. Cheryl is one of the most generous people I know. She gives of herself to her family, friends, and community through her music, laughter, twinkling eyes, and presence. As a leader, she recognizes that the investment she makes of her gifts and talents in the lives of those who rely on her gives her the energy she needs to continue giving. Rather than seeing the demands on her time as distractions, Cheryl uses them to energize herself, transforming both the person whose need she meets and herself in the process.

How often do we respond with impatience or irritation when what is needed is instruction or information? How much more of a transformation in thought, behavior, or attitude can we make when we see opportunity instead of imposition? Remember those times you did something, seemingly simple, for another person and watched his face light up in appreciation? Remember the corresponding smile that gradually appeared on your own face in response?

Energy! Giving! Try it next time and notice the transformation in yourself and in the other person.

You have a touch of destiny in you, Tia Dalma in *Pirates of the Caribbean: Dead Man's Chest.*

I love this line from the movie. It can be said of anyone.

If we have destiny in us, it means we have purpose, hope, a plan for our lives. The beauty is that we get to decide our destiny. We are the only ones who control our intention. We are the only ones who control our response to the circumstances and events that happen all around us. You determine your course of action, whether by creating a new pathway or following an established one.

We all have a touch of destiny in us. Not in the sense of a preordered path or life over which we have little to no control. In the sense that we are here to fulfill purpose, to have meaning and to live a life that is impactful .... Our existence makes a difference. Our lives are transactional and, if we allow, transformational.

I hope you, as a leader, choose to forge a new path, build a new highway where there was none, create a trail out of forest and weeds. Leave a way that is clear and as stumble-free as possible for those who follow, so that when they reach the end of your path, they have the energy and inspiration to break off in yet another new direction of discovery and growth. This is living with purpose and meaning. This is fulfilling your destiny.

Timing is more important than time.

I don't know where I saw or heard this one, so apologies in advance to the author. The reason it's included is that when people are depending on you, for whatever reasons, how long or how much of your time is invested with them isn't nearly as critical as the timing.

Trying to teach a concept to students at the wrong time is a wasted effort, no matter how much time you spend, workbooks you buy, tutors you hire, or punishing/rewarding you do. Every educator knows that until the student has the foundational grasp and is academically ready for the "next step," learning just won't happen. It's a matter of timing.

I had a special needs high school student, "Paul," who was 19, could not read, and was classified as developmentally challenged with emotional dysfunction ... In plain English, Paul didn't "get it" like other students, so along the line, he was just moved from grade to grade, until finally, he was tested and placed in special education – when he was in seventh grade (grrr, don't get me started)! Anyway, by the time he came to me, he'd been in high school for four years and, according to the state law then, could remain until age 21.

Paul was angry, sometimes sullen, mistrusting, and prickly. It took me a few weeks to figure out that he liked, and was good at, jigsaw puzzles. That also told me something; he was capable of learning to read. Now, I just had to figure out the right method and timing. Watching Paul work his puzzles gave me the answer. He determined where a piece should go by tracing the edges of the piece using his fingers and eyes, then by tracing the spaces of the in-progress puzzle. I watched him select a piece, feel and study the possible placements, only to put it down, do the same with a new piece and without hesitation, put it in place.

After watching and thinking for several days I was ready. I brought a small jar of sand to class, pulled out some good old Elmer's Glue and cut up pieces of poster board. After getting everyone else settled and on task, I walked over to Paul's table. "Paul?" I asked. "May I interrupt you for a moment?" Without looking up, he responded, "Yes, Miss gillie."

"I'd like to do a new kind of puzzle with you. Will you work it with me?" That got his attention! He looked up at me holding the supplies, his eyes expectant. I sat beside him, away from the in-process puzzle. Taking the glue, I squeezed the letters of his name on the poster board, sprinkled sand over the glue, and shook off the extra.

"May I have your finger, Paul?" I asked as he reached his hand forward, eyes on the poster board. "This puzzle is made of letter pieces and the pieces together make a word. I'm going to let you feel the letters as I tell you what they are and what word they make." Holding his finger, I traced it slowly over the letters while saying them out loud.

One time. That's all it took. Once. His eyes lit up when I said, "Paul." "My name," he said. "That puzzle is me," he continued; pulled his hand out of mine and without hesitation, spelled each letter as he traced it and proudly announced, "Paul." I figured he just memorized the word. Then, he asked for another word puzzle, so I took the glue and another piece of poster board and "wrote" the word "all." As soon as I shook off the extra sand, Paul traced the letters, saying each one correctly, then looked at me expectantly, "all," I provided. "all," he said and trace/spelled it again. "More please, Miss gillie?" he asked. Using all the poster board I'd cut up, I made word puzzles, reviewing once or twice, then left him to it. Timing. Nothing more. Nothing less. Timing is me figuring out the puzzle ability, timing in using the sand, timing in having gained the trust of a child who didn't like to be touched. Timing.

It's almost never what you think it is; and usually what you think it isn't.

Assumptions get him in trouble every time. He's the kind of guy almost everyone has in their life. Opinionated. Loud. Arrogant. Often rude and condescending. My buddy, Susan Amat, calls them "jerks." I agree. He was also my boss.

This particular time, he was doing my performance appraisal. We were sitting in his office and he was doing his usual "harassment leer" at me when he said, "I'm looking at a million dollars right there, and I'm not getting my money's worth from you, joyce." He was always making comments, giving me the "up-and-down" look, standing too close. I ignored, walked away or moved away. Not interested … at all! For one, he was a jerk. Two, I was married with a son. Three, he was a jerk. This time, he was being direct and threatening. "I'm not in sales, 'William'. That's what Jack and Henry do. I'm a project manager and work with the clients they bring in," I responded calmly as I met his eyes.

William reared back in his oversized leather chair and grinned, "If you want to keep this job, you don't have any choice about giving me what I expect from you." See, he assumed that he knew what I would do. A young wife and mother who was the primary source of income for her family, I would "give him what he wanted," in his mind. "Besides," he continued. "You don't have any other choice."

Gathering the notes I'd brought and my copy of the review – which was horrible, in spite of my stellar performance – I stood. In that moment, I remembered that there were family members and friends of the family who would help and support me. I remembered the lessons I'd learned about making choices. I remembered that I and only I could respond to situations in ways that taught others how I would be treated …. I smiled, as I rose to my feet. "I *always* have choices, William," I said. Then I turned and walked out.

It didn't go the way he thought it would then and when I turned in my resignation to accept another, better job in a different state a few weeks later, it certainly wasn't what he thought would happen.

Everyone leaves a legacy.
What will your legacy be?

Thom has an old poster hanging on the wall in our garage. It shows a huge pile of "stuff." The caption says, "Whoever has the most things when he dies ... wins." It's a reminder to me that I never want my legacy to be that I had a lot of stuff when I die. I want it to be the transformational impact I had on the lives of people I encountered. I want it to be the difference I made in them. I want it to be my reputation for always trying to be better, to improve. I want to leave a legacy of leadership that lasts far beyond my own life. What will your legacy be?

Life is like a box of chocolates; you never know what you're going to get,
Forrest Gump.

When you know and respect your own Inner Nature, you know where you belong. You also know where you don't belong, Benjamin Hoff. and *No matter how Useful we may be, sometimes it takes us a while to recognize our own value,* Benjamin Hoff.
One of my favorite protégés called me and said, "Things have changed at [her workplace] and I don't fit any more." "Tell me why," I responded. She proceeded to tell me about the nepotism, cronyism, and willingness to "cut corners" that had been developing. She talked about the way her position was being undermined and sabotaged; how her activities were suddenly being monitored; how she was being asked to clock in, even though she was a

salaried, not hourly, employee. She was describing a workplace where she no longer belonged.

We talked for a long time. Discussed some possible champions she could reach out to. Talked about exit strategies and opportunities. In the end, none of that mattered. She was forced out. Fair? No. Just? Again, no. Right? Still, no. Yet, the reality was what it was. She knows her inner self. She knows what works for her. She knows when it doesn't. She moved on to a workplace that gave her what she needed to thrive.

Why did it happen? I believe it was because the Manager had no idea what his own inner nature was and became threatened by hers. She was becoming the "face" of the organization, not him. She was the one that other employees went to when they had problems to solve or issues to fix, not him. She received the invitations and requests for appearances, not him. Because he wasn't self-aware, he became resentful. Like animals when cornered, he attacked.

She knew her value and knew when it wasn't valued in return. That allowed her to have the courage to move on. Wiser. Stronger. Better than before. Today, she's looking at another opportunity. Weighing the pros and the cons. I know that she's ready. I'm just waiting for her to recognize it (smile).

As transformative leaders, we can't afford to not be self-aware. We must take the time to figure out *who* we are and *why* we feel and behave as we do. Otherwise, we'll never end up where we belong, doing what we should ... and neither can those who follow us.

A void is always filled. You decide what fills it.

Never compare your own insides to someone else's outside, Carole Sager.

We all make comparisons. Hair. Possessions. Clothing and Style. Positions and Power. We usually think that external changes will bring internal improvements.

Every time I see a commercial for external products, I remember this quote. Using that shampoo, moisturizer, hair coloring, or clothing isn't going to change a single fundamental aspect of my character. It won't make me happier or kinder. "Pretty is as pretty does," is the saying many of us grew up hearing. The older I get, the more I discover its truth.

On the outside, he looks totally put together. He must have it all. What you don't see is that he has a developmentally challenged child, a father who no longer knows who he is, a wife who has been having an affair for years, a sister in drug rehab … again, and another child who is on suicide watch. Yet, if you just look at him, without ever getting to know his life, you might be envious when you consider your own insides. That would be a mistake. We never know the life burdens that others are carrying. Comparing ourselves only to what we see is not the comparison to make. Until we see and know the inside, we know nothing about a person and will only end up frustrated and angry with ourselves and with our lives.

You can accept or reject the way you are treated by other people, but until you heal the wounds of your past, you will continue to bleed, Iyanla Vanzant. and *As years pass, and the abundance of the future is depleted, the crux of old mistakes and the cost of old choices are ever recalibrated,* Gregory Maguire.

There are periods in our lives when we don't want to think about or even remember choices we made, actions we took, or pathways we followed. They're too painful. As with many things, distance brings perspective. Most of the time we eventually get to a point when we can look back. We can reflect. We can consider the myriad of ways we arrived where we currently are in life.

We can eventually begin to consider that we are who we are and we're doing what we're doing, precisely because of our choices. We can begin to see those choices not as mistakes; instead, we begin to see them as necessary for teaching us what we need for today. Those hardships prepared us for what we will need tomorrow. That reality is librating. Forgiving. Accepting the person we have become with the realization that we have not only survived; we have thrived because of what we've been through.

There was a long hard time when I kept far from me the remembrance of what I had thrown away when I was quite ignorant of its worth, Charles Dickens.

If you erase all of your bad memories, you erase all of your wisdom, Matshona Dhliwayo.

We learn so much from our failures. We are changed more too. Why then do so many try to erase them? Shouldn't we celebrate them for the lessons they gave and the transformations they created? Shouldn't we do the same organizationally?

In the medical profession, after the death of a patient, frequently, the medical staff have what is called an M & M – Morbidity and Mortality conference. They review, ask questions about, and discuss every aspect of the case being presented. The doctors, technicians, and nurses go over every detail to see if something could be done better or a new protocol should be in place. Why don't we do that in the nonmedical world? How much could we transform our organizations if we did M & M on the proposals not accepted or jobs unsuccessfully completed? Shouldn't we buy doughnuts and coffee, call everyone involved together, and dissect what happened? Sounds like a great practice. Who's with me?

Do not let the memories of your past limit the potential of your future. There are no limits to what you can achieve on your journey through life, except in your mind, Roy T. Bennett.

I think that somehow, we learn who we really are and then live with that decision, Eleanor Roosevelt.

Learning who we really are can be painful. Living with the knowledge of who we are can be freeing.

Aviva Dawn has experienced more than her share of loss and hardship, beginning at a very young age. Starting with the loss of a parent and eventually becoming a newly single mom. Life threw her curve ball after curve ball. Through it all, she stumbled her way forward. Always seeking answers and opportunities. Never giving up. Discovering and living with herself.

Today, she knows who she is and what she is here to do. She is a mother, daughter, sister, aunt, and friend to those of us who are fortunate enough to love her. She is budding filmmaker, a poet, and a brilliant writer. She is a survivor. She is thriving. She is becoming who she is meant to be. She thrives within the decision of who she is. I'm proud of her and honored to have known and loved the girl she was, and to know and love the woman she is becoming, as she continues her self-transformation.

What you resist not only persists, but will continue to grow in size, Carl Jung.

Confession time! I hate going through the seemingly long, slow, agonizing process of learning life lessons. I mean, really … can't we just skip that part and get to the end? Like you can skip pages in a book or fast forward for a movie or show? Why not?!?!

Okay, another confession. I've tried that. It. Doesn't. Work. The more I try to shortcut the life lessons, the longer they take. The harder and more painful they become. The further away the end seems to be. Eventually, at some point in my life, I stopped resisting. I also became better at encouraging those who choose to follow me. Life lessons!

The only true wisdom is in knowing you know nothing, Socrates, by attribution.

The first step in crafting the life you want is to get rid of everything you don't, Joshua Becker.

She was spiraling out of control. Crashing into walls of self-destruction. Fracturing relationships and opportunities. Lost, without direction. Her mother, my friend, didn't know what to do … let her daughter self-destruct or fight to save her? At the very bottom of her self-built pit, she woke up. Took stock. Then set about slowly, painfully clawing her way back to the surface. We all helped her.

When she emerged, she looked back, then filled in the gaping pit of what was her former life with purpose, direction, clarity, honesty, dependability, resilience, and courage. She threw away everything that had held her back and strangled her, and moved toward the life she wanted … and deserved.

Do you know someone who is spiraling or lost? Are you trying to "help" by fixing the messes or solving the problems? Don't! As hard and as terrifying as it is to watch, until she is ready to build the life she wants, until she throws away everything holding her back; you're just prolonging the struggle. It seems counterintuitive, doesn't it? Feels like if we help her out of one more "mess" she'll see the light and realize what she needs to do. Here's the thing. It's *not* about you, it's about her (or him). It's about her choices and dealing with the consequences that teaches the lessons to be learned. If you alleviate the consequences ….

She has to decide that she doesn't like the life she's created. *She* has to decide that she wants to build a new one. *She* has to decide to change. *She* has to decide to throw away the old. *She* has to decide that she's ready for transformation. Until then, all you can do, the best thing you can do, is wait.

The moment one definitely commits oneself, then Providence moves as well. All sorts of things occur to help one that would never otherwise have occurred. A stream of events issues from the decision, raising in one's favor all manner of unforeseen accidents, meetings, and material assistance that no one could have dreamed would come their way. Whatever you can do or dream you can do, begin it. Boldness has genius, power, and magic in it. Begin it now, Goethe, by attribution.

As I look back over the pathways of my life, I realize how true this is. Once I decided, all kinds of options became available; just like the emergency lights on a plane. You never see the lights until you need them. The hardest thing is to make the decision to move without seeing the lights. The easiest thing is looking back and realizing they were always there.

WHEN TIMES ARE HARD...

loss, pain, failure, disappointment

To be yourself in a world that is constantly trying to make you something else is the greatest accomplishment, Ralph Waldo Emerson.

Thom will tell anyone that his primary goal has always been, "To be free." He wanted to chart his own course, not have some corporate manager do it for him. He wanted to be able to pursue the things that gave him joy ... writing, acting, leading, consulting, communicating, transforming.

He quickly realized that he wasn't going to be able to do that at Bell South (now AT & T). His career goal was, "to be President," and when he was told in the 1980s that he couldn't, with no reason given, that was when he decided to do it on his own. He founded *Thom Gossom Communications* in May 1987 (later becoming today's *Best Gurl, inc.*). He was, finally, "President" Today, he's the CEO of Best Gurl, inc. He has remained true to himself the entire way. Transforming people and organizations. Helping others to realize their own greatest achievements. Making a difference, even when it was hard.

Whether through death/loss or life/gain, we experience the five-stage grieving process with change.

This means we should be gentle with ourselves and with others through the Denial/Shock, Anger, Blame/Bargaining, and Depression/Despondence until we reach Acceptance. Major change requires longer periods of time to process the emotions and reach Acceptance, especially dealing with death.

We avoid really dealing with death in the US, we don't even call it "death" – we come up with words and phrases as though that will lessen the blow felt by those left behind. Regardless of your culture or beliefs about the after-death experience or existence, the truth remains that the only way we leave this world is through our death and there is so much we could do to support each other, yet, in my experience, too often we don't. Perhaps because we don't want to think about what it will be like when we face the death of a significant person in our lives; perhaps because we don't want to think about our own death or loss. Whatever the reason, it's not about you … it's about the person most closely connected to the loss and their feelings of denial, anger, blame, and depression. Telling him to "be strong" makes him feel that when he wants to blame the doctor or loved one, that something is wrong with him. The biggest reason we often think we are the only one to experience certain emotions or thoughts is that almost no one talks about or admits having them! So here it is, the conversations about death that almost no one wants to have that applies to other types of change as well.

Don't expect him to make any major decisions at least for the first year (job, move, sell the house, etc.). Psychologists and behaviorists will tell you that our brain isn't really functioning on all cylinders during that time. It makes me wish we still adhered to some of the Victorian era nobility customs for mourning and it makes me understand why they were practiced. During the first year, those who were closest to the deceased weren't expected to do anything or go anywhere. Others handled social commitments, the household was taken care of by family, friends, and neighbors. During the second year, things that were "light" were gradually resumed, and by the third year, there was an increase in social and household activities. By that time, it was less "raw" and the mourners mind was "fuzzy" less often. Makes a lot of sense, doesn't it? Much better than what we try to do now … "jump back in as quickly as possible" and "be strong." Makes absolutely no sense to me!

Please don't tell her anything like, "Your loved one is in a better place," because here is what she is thinking. "There is no better place for my mother/husband/child than with me" and you're just making her angrier and sadder because she can't say that to you. Also, don't say "The Lord never gives us more than we can handle," because that is not how she feels right now. At this moment/week/year, she feels like her entire world has exploded into millions of pieces and she has no idea where to begin or what to do. Another one is, "Try to look for the good in the situation. Be positive." Seriously, and just what is she supposed to be positive about … not having to take care of her sick child any longer, not having to travel to check on her dad? Think about what you're saying and don't ….

Perhaps, one of the worst things you can say is "I know how you feel" or "I miss him just as much as you do." We never really know how someone else feels and both tend to make many grievers angry (angrier). Eventually, he will be ready to hear about how much you also miss the one who has died, but not right now and not until he initiates or asks. You just need to listen. That's pretty much it for a long, long time. As soon as you start to talk or relate the death to yourself, he will probably stop talking, and may never come back to you to share his feelings. It's hard to just listen … and this is one of those times when silence is the best answer.

In an episode of the television series, *New Amsterdam*, an 18-year old was told that the cancer he'd battled for three years earlier in his life had returned. He made the decision not to tell his parents or anyone else. Instead, he was going to leave school and travel, fall in love, and do as many other things as possible that he had missed out on during his early teen years. He was given 4-6 months. Explaining his decision, he said, "My death is going to be awful for my parents either way; whether I tell them now or not. At least this way, it won't be awful for me." Initially, we would think of this young man as "selfish." Yet, isn't loss and death the ultimate act of selfishness? We leave those who love us behind. We move on to another city, job, afterlife, whatever …. Those who remain, or are affected by the change, grieve.

So, what *should* we say to the griever? Try any of these that feel comfortable to you. "I don't know what to say." "There are no words to make this better for you." "I will listen if you need someone to talk to." "I know I can't fix it. I just want you to know I care." "Please be gentle with yourself and know that whatever you're feeling is okay." "You don't have to be anything for anybody, just be what you feel." "It just isn't fair." Above all, hold him when he needs holding and give him tissues when he needs to cry.

If we all threw our problems in a pile and saw everyone else's, we'd grab ours back, Regina Brett.

I look at this whenever I start to feel whiny and sorry for myself. Mentally, I go through the lives of people with whom I am friendly, a colleague or friend of, or related to. When I sit quietly and reflect, my mental hand reaches out and eases my problems back to my side. Honestly, I don't know that I could – and I know I don't want to – handle what many of those in my tribes struggle with daily.

If I'm really sliding into a funk, a mental comparison list is required. Headache, cancer. Tired, driving 500 miles in a day. Hungry, homeless. Paying bills, jobless with four dependents. Lost a client, lost a spouse. Too many emails, anxiety attack. Yeah, that slows my roll ... waaay down.

On the very rare occasion when neither of those can pull me out of myself, it's time for the big guns ... "Hi, I was thinking about you and wanted you to know I love you. How are you?" Sometimes, an hour or more later, I hang up. Usually tearful and never, ever focused on myself.

It's not what you go through that defines you, you can't help that. It's what you do AFTER you've gone through it that really tests who you are, Kwame Floyd.

There once was a young man, not long out of grad school, who we hired. He was outgoing, innovative, and had endless potential. I eventually took him on as a protégé, which I rarely do because, for me, it is a lifetime commitment to him or her. Over time and through observation, I identified the gaps in his skill set and experience. Projects and responsibilities were assigned that would give him opportunities to learn, fail, succeed, and grow. At the same time, I was seeing and learning who he really was (remember relationships?), so I decided it was time for his final challenge opportunity. He, and I, needed to know if he really was up to the task of leading.

Having the conversation to tell him about his new assignment, it was obvious he didn't like it. That, I expected. What I wanted to find out was how he would handle it. That would tell me who he really was and whether he could successfully lead. So, I remained firm and observed his actions.

I wish I could give you a "happy ending."

He used all the positive abilities and the skills he learned during our years together to help bring about, what he thought was, a solidification of power for personal gain. He operated with no regard for the impact on others and lacked the strategic visioning to even see the ultimate impact on himself. Needless to say, he brought about his own professional downfall … and I allowed it. Not because I was angry, although I was very disappointed. I allowed it because we can only know who we are after we have been put to a test. Whether we rise up or chose to sink low, we know who we are. That knowledge gives us an opportunity to reflect, and if we sank low, to adjust and modify our patterns of behavior. It was a hard lesson to experience for him. As the leader, it was even harder for me to deliver.

I hope that, wherever he is today, he has reflected and modified his patterns. And that he is a better leader because of it.

People get what they think they deserve.

She creates her own reality, and impacts the reality of those around her, from her own beliefs and thoughts. When she has doubt. When she is brave.

When she is insecure. When she is confident. Her thoughts direct her responses to others as well. If she expects to be overlooked or discounted, she will be. If she believes that she isn't respected, she won't be. If she knows that others will respond positively toward her, they most often will.

Mastering our own "self-speak" to eliminate or silence the negative and enhance or encourage the positive is an important gift we can give ourselves and those who follow us. I don't mean telling myself that I'm 5'2" when I'm not and never will be. I mean, reminding myself that I have everything I need for today when I start to worry about money or clients. It also means reminding myself that I am loved and important when someone I lead is upset with or fussing at me. Reminding myself that while he is upset now, once he calms down and thinks about whatever it is, he'll realize that there was no way I would have intentionally hurt him. So, I can be calm, listen, and wait until we can laugh about this experience some day.

The pleasure of remembering had been taken from me, because there was no longer anyone to remember with. It felt like losing your co-rememberer meant losing the memory itself, as if the things we'd done were less real and important than they had been hours before, John Green.

There are so many times I want to relive and talk about a special time, place, meal, whatever … only to realize that the only person who shares that memory with me is gone. Those memories, over time, have become more and more difficult to reflect on and accurately remember. Whether it is a professional achievement or a personal experience, we need the shared memory of others who had the experience with us if we are to fully immerse ourselves in the pleasure of remembering. Look for ways to keep special events and occasions alive through shared memories with multiple people. Create new memories for anyone you lead and include as many people as possible in the creation. That way, when you are no longer in that place or position, they, the memory – and the feelings with them – will continue.

A woman is like a tea bag – you can't tell how strong she is until you put her in hot water, Eleanor Roosevelt.

I've been in hot water more often than I would have liked (laughing). Job loss. Client loss. Deaths of loved ones. Financial hardships. Employee theft. Broken relationships. The list could go on endlessly.

Know what I've learned, though? I'm strong. I'm resilient. I'm courageous. I'm determined. I'm still standing. So are you.

It's so much darker when a light is lost than it would have been if it had never shone, John Steinbeck.

Our eyes take so much longer to adjust when we're in a room and turn the light off than they do going into a room with no light at all.

Grief is such a beast. It tears your life into shreds, and you end up becoming nothing more than tattered pieces of who you used to be.

As I'm working on this book, the world, and the US where I live, is gripped by and struggling with one of the worst pandemics in history. More than a million people have died worldwide. Millions have been and are infected. People are quarantined. Sheltering and working from home. At the same time, there are hundreds of thousands, perhaps even millions of people protesting the killing of men and women of color, mostly black or African American people, especially by police all over the US. Globally and nationally people's lives are in tatters. Poverty and unemployment levels are rising. Hospitals are overcrowded and many have begun turning away those who are not critically ill. Protesters, police, and property are being attacked. People are shattered, depressed, and anxious. Suicide levels are increasing. There is global turmoil.

In so many ways, whatever you want to call it, people are grieving. What can a transformative leader do in the face of so much? Lead. Listen. Realize where people are emotionally, and do *everything* within your power to give those who choose to follow you the reassurances you have within your power to give. Help them shift into the new paradigm of normal. Let them work safely from home whenever possible. Provide safe work spaces for those who cannot work from home. Assess your own organization to identify areas that lack diversity, integrity, or are non-inclusive. Listen to the voices of everyone in the organization you lead, not just the ones you want to hear. Make changes. Do more than make a public statement. Change the way your organization, looks, acts, and operates. People's lives are shattered. They need you to step up and lead.

Nothing on earth can make up for the loss of one who has loved you, Selma Lagerlöf.

I can't tell you how many times I either deleted this quote or decided to leave it without reflection. In the end, I had to stay true to my purpose, leave it in, and share my thoughts.

If you are among the fortunate, you have that one person in your life who loves you unconditionally. It may be a parent, spouse, child, or friend. You know with absolute certainty that no matter how unlovingly you behave or what mistakes you make, she will continue to love you and be kind to you even if she disagrees with you. When that person is gone ... whether through death or other life circumstances, you are cast adrift. There is nothing and no one who can take her place. No one else who fits just right. No one you can completely feel safe with. I know. I'm living that castaway life. Perhaps you are as well. Perhaps someone in your life is living it. Don't feel that you're not important to him; you are. Don't feel that you can replace the one who loved him; you can't. All you can do is be present. Be steadfast. Be as consistent as possible as he works his way into his new "normal."

There is no quota on misery for people, no quantifiable threshold that once reached, got you miraculously taken out of the distress pool, J.R. Ward.

If you can fix it, replace it, do it over, or do without, it's not worth worrying about.

Instead of spending energy and time worrying, invest it in fixing what can be fixed, going to get another one, starting over again, or moving on. In reality, the only thing that doesn't fit into one of those four categories is life itself. That's the only thing you have, absolutely, no ability to fix, replace, or do over. Everything else … Spilled coffee, fix it. Lost your job, replace it. Failed relationship, fix it, do without, or replace it. Disgruntled customer, fix or replace them. See what I mean? Almost anything you can think of can be fixed, replaced, done over, or done without. Yet, we spend so much energy, time, and sometimes money, worrying about whatever it is, that we lose sight of what we can do. Focus on that … not the worrying!

THE ART OF WAR ... ACCORDING TO SUN TZU

strategy and philosophy

Don't fight, win. The supreme art of war is to subdue the enemy without fighting, Sun Tzu. and *If an injury has been made to a man it should be so severe that his vengeance need not be feared,* Niccolo Machiavelli.

Or, to more accurately quote Sun Tzu, "Win before you fight," create a situation that almost guarantees that you are mentally, physically, and financially assured of the outcome. Then, wait for the timing that gives you the best possible advantage for the outcome you seek. Make sure that this is not only something *worth* fighting for, make sure you can get what you need. Watch for the mistakes made by others and use them to the advantage of reaching your goal. Perhaps most important; know, feel, see, smell, and taste what success is for the situation. If you can't describe it for everyone following you into "battle," don't start the fight! If you do decide to fight, make sure you finish it so thoroughly there is no possible chance of retaliation. Otherwise, you will always be looking over your shoulder.

Women do a lot of good, with not a lot of fuss, Michelle Anchors.

This describes Michelle perfectly! She is a transformative leader in every sense of the word. Let me tell you a story ….

Several years ago, Michelle discovered an organization, Impact100 Global. The concept is simple *and* radical. Establish as a 501(c)3, find at least 100 women (only), ask each woman to give $1000, vet and select a game-changing nonprofit organization project, give them the $100,000 to implement that project … transform a community! Michelle loved that every penny of the money given by Impact100 women went to the nonprofit. Her attorney side approved of the rigorous financial and organizational vetting process and that a Board Member works with the nonprofit during the two-year project implementation, instead of just writing a check. As a leader, Michelle recognized something that could, indeed, transform our community … and it has.

With little fuss or fanfare, Michelle systematically approached women in our two-county area; sharing the model and asking them to become founding Board Members. I don't know of anyone who told her, "no." After filing for and getting 501(c)3 status approval, and other legal documents, those initial women started reaching out to everyone they knew. In our first year, Impact100 of Northwest Florida had 128 members who donated $1000 each and gave a $128,000 Grant to "Safe Connections" to purchase and renovate a house that could be used as a secure and safe place for family visitation with abused or neglected children. Selected from the five grant areas, there wasn't a dry eye when Safe Connections was announced as the recipient after member voting. Michelle's "no fuss" method has resulted in more than a $3.1 million investment for nonprofits through Impact100 of Northwest Florida so far. That's a *lot* of good and very little fuss. It's what transformational leadership should do. Thanks, Michelle!

Follow the Money ...

I didn't make it up, and I don't know (or care) who did. What I do know is that if you want to understand the "why" of many, many decisions or actions, just follow the money. What does it have to do with transformational leadership? If you know who will either make or lose money depending on the outcome of a decision you want to make you can avoid hassle, delays, conniving, or denial if you deal with the money first. When you fail to do that, you can almost guarantee your failure.

Let's talk the common cold ... everyone gets them at some point or another, even babies and seniors. We're told that there is no "cure" because it's viral, not bacterial, and that it has to "run its course." However, there are hundreds of products you can buy over-the-counter that will, "help the symptoms" of a cold.

Researchers tell us that there are 200 or so strains of the rhinovirus that cause the common cold (*Scientific American*) and that it would be cost-prohibitive to develop a vaccine for all of them. Some researchers are trying to identify a common viral structure, and develop a vaccine for each structure. Still others are working on a "cocktail" mixture common cold vaccine, like the vaccines for polio or pneumonia. The common cold costs the US economy billions of dollars a year – lost productivity and time at work, doctor visits, over the counter medicines, and antibiotics (*Stanford Medicine*). According to *The Guardian*, current academic, government and pharmaceutical funding isn't enough. To effectively continue the promising results already at hand it would require several years and at least $1B (*The Guardian*).

So, why would pharmaceutical company leaders invest the millions of dollars to develop, test, and get approval for a drug that might cure something that currently earns them a *guaranteed* $23.2 Billion (as of 2018, *Businesswire*) in over the counter and antibiotic medications?! Who is going to invest money in a vaccine for billions of people that could destroy a multibillion-dollar industry and will probably never pay for itself …?

Rare is the leader who will go up against the money, especially that kind of money. Whether or not you agree with the outcome, take the time to follow the money before deciding whether or not it is a situation you want to take on.

You can run far and you can run fast, but you can't outrun your upbringing,
Paul Schrader.

Good or not so good. Values or questionable values. Integrity or not so much. Dependability, honesty, pushing through fear, resilience, follow-through, cleaning up after yourself, self-reliance; and so many more. Even when we try to be "like other people," during crisis and inconvenienced times, the character that was forged during our upbringing too often shines forth.

As a leader, keep in mind, that isn't always a good thing.

I know and care about someone I follow; let's call her "Pam," who has come from modest socioeconomic conditions. She and her family always had "just enough." There were definite values and morals taught in the household as well as some not so great characteristics that have created large and small stumbling blocks for her.

During disagreements or arguments, Pam describes a lot of yelling and ugly things being said. "I didn't know that everyone wasn't that way," she told me once. "That's just what we did. You blew up, got it off your chest, then it was over and everyone was good again." She chuckled and shook her head, "Imagine how I felt when I blew up at my roommate after she left our room light on for the third time. She walked out, then came back with the RA to file a report against me. I had no idea what I'd even done wrong!"

Pam was stunned to learn that letting things fester, not saying anything "To be nice," she said, only to reach the tipping point and explode, was not the way other people handled disagreements. "She didn't even fight back," Pam chuckles now, "She just left. You're supposed to yell back. Hash it out. Then be over it and move on. At least, that's what I thought," she says, with a grimace. "Not only did my roommate file an official complaint with the Residence Hall Assistant, she requested, and got, a room change!"

During her years in college, Pam slowly began to change her way of dealing with conflict. She describes the way she worked hard to say something, calmly, when the other person did something she didn't like or appreciate. "It was hard, really hard," she says. "I'd do well one time, then blow up the next three or four times," she laughs. "I lost so many relationships." Eventually, in the workplace, Pam got better at responding. Until one fateful day she will never forget.

"I was a new supervisor and one of my direct reports was always late for meetings," Pam's eyes fill with tears as she talks. "He came into a staff meeting, all smiles, shrugs, and 'I'm sorry'," she continues. "I'd had it and exploded all over him. Ugly, horrible words spilled out of my mouth. Not just about being late, but also about projects he'd mishandled, reports he hadn't done correctly; everything I hadn't said because I wanted to be a good boss, I wanted him to like me. It was like all of the air was sucked out of the room," she continues. Looking at me, she whispered, "They looked at me like I was a monster. Everyone. The whole room. I realized that I'd done it ... again. Held on to things that should have been said calmly, rationally. Instead, I behaved just like my family; only these people weren't family, they were employees and they weren't going to fight back, they couldn't. I was their boss, so what could they do? What could they say? Nothing."

"My boss Richard, the department manager, came in. He looked at my staff, sitting in shock and disgust. He looked at Jeremy, the man I'd yelled at. Finally, he looked at me and said, 'Pam come with me please.' As I followed him out of the conference room, I looked at Jeremy and whispered, 'I'm so sorry!' He nodded, but his eyes were unforgiving. Hard and angry. I headed to Richard's office following behind him." Pam pauses and takes a deep breath.

"He fired me. On the spot," Pam continues. "Richard said that that kind of harassment would not be and was not tolerated. He told me to clear my office and meet him in HR and that I had 15 minutes. I wish I could say that was the last time I exploded. It wasn't," she goes on, struggling with embarrassment. "Employees, friends, husband, children. Even salespeople and service personnel. I'd do so well for a while, then I'd explode. I finally realized that I'd never 'get past it;' that it was part of me, like my upbringing. It has, and always will be, my struggle to overcome the way I was raised," Pam concludes.

I couldn't argue with her. Especially in times of conflict or stress in terms of our character, we tend to revert to our "roots." We do what we saw or experienced when we were growing up. Whether that's blowing up in anger, like Pam, or resorting to distance and silence, like me; we're all a product of our environment. You really can run far and fast, and still in some ways, never outrun how you were raised. That means, we need to own it and recognize it whenever our upbringing interferes with us being effective leaders. Whenever it gets in the way of what we *should* be giving to others that transforms them.

Nothing is ever settled until it is settled right, Rudyard Kipling.

I will confront another form of bias: the soft bigotry of low expectations, George W. Bush.

Not every battle is an obvious one. This was very eloquently expressed by, then candidate Bush, during an address to the National Association for the Advancement of Colored People (NAACP) at the national convention in 2000. It is a perfect description of how certain groups of people are held to a lower standard; therefore, preventing growth, advancement, and progress toward an otherwise obtainable goal.

Do you make allowance for certain followers? Do you overlook grammar, language or word use, dress, behavior, educational achievement, and more? If so, have you ever stopped to ask yourself why? As a leader, have you found yourself only giving the challenging or difficult projects or assignments to particular people, and never to others? Why? As a teacher, do you grade the work of some students more rigorously than others? Why? As a parent, do you have higher expectation for one or more of your children than their siblings? Again …. Why? "The soft bigotry of low expectations." That's why.

Even when/if we aren't aware of the existence, this form of bias permeates our decisions and actions. We, unconsciously sometimes, make "allowances" for the behaviors, or lack of, in others, thinking, "She's doing the best she can," or "I don't want to push him too hard and discourage him," or worse, "If I point this out, it may make her feel like she isn't good enough (trying hard enough) and she'll stop trying completely." Yet, don't we also hear, see, and know that humans are capable of so, so much more than we think they are?

I often find myself either temporarily, sometimes permanently, at odds with someone I care deeply about when I point out (call out) a shortcoming or behavior. Something they know, deep inside, isn't the best cause of action, decision, or thing to say. They'd prefer that I remain silent. Overlook it. Not say anything. I won't. Ever. Anytime. Even when it's my turn to be called on my shortcomings. I hate it. Makes me furious with myself. And I so badly need it if I'm going to grow.

I want to always challenge myself … and those for whom I am responsible or care about. Yes, it may make her angry and she might stop speaking to me. Yes, it may make him cut me out of his life. Yes, it can cause a jagged tear in an otherwise wonderful relationship. Yes, and … the truth will be known; the expectation will be maintained; the growth is still possible; the excuses are nullified; and I am true to myself and to him or her. So is the person who is willing to give me the same.

No one ever said that leadership was easy. There is no guarantee that everyone will *want* to follow you. Not everyone will enjoy being held accountable. At the same time, if a leader cannot or will not be loved by her followers, then Machiavelli tells us that she should work toward being feared.

Be careful about the advice you get … be even more careful about the advice you give.

I hate the phrase, "May I give you some unsolicited advice?". My answer is usually, "No, thank you." (laughing) Why? Because, too often – not always

– the speaker is the *most* unqualified person to successfully advise me. Those who are in my "inner circle" already know that they don't need to ask first. Their advice is always valued, even if I don't like knowing I need the advice. Ditto for those whose inner circle I'm in. For everyone else, "You have to walk the talk to earn the right to be heard." So, make sure that you are (or the person is) a walking, talking, living example of the advice you're (they're) about to give … otherwise, you (they) should sit down and be quiet!

Because sometimes people who seem good end up being not as good as you might have hoped, Jonathan Safran Foer.

Lack of planning on your part does not constitute an emergency on mine.
Al, the Quality Assurance Manager at the Georgia Power E.I. Hatch Plant; taught me that most valuable lesson. Over the years, I've found myself using this one often. With others. Even more with myself.

Just because something is legal, doesn't mean it's the right thing to do.
Not warning a stranger about a dangerous situation.

Paying minimum wage to full-time employees.

Only asking women to plan or shop for office functions and events.

Marketing $200 shoes to teens who live in poverty.

Throwing materials that could be recycled into the trash; throwing trash into the recycle bin.

Not building full-service grocery stores in working income neighborhoods.

Working with foreign suppliers who have poor employee safety practices.

Giving high profile projects or assignments only to men.

Selling high-calorie food in small quantity packaging at higher prices in low income communities.

Serving low nutrition food, instead of fresh fruit and vegetables, to school children because it's less expensive.

Leaving a mess (or an empty anything) for someone else to clean up or refill.

Interrupting while the other person is talking ... busy ... thinking ....

Offering high-cost loans that have daily compounded interest.

Lying ... breaking a promise ... not doing what you said ....

Terminating an employee with no notice for vague, or no good, reason.

All are legal. Are any of them the best for the affected people? That's the real question ... and the real issue.

You can't control anything in life other than your response to what happens around you ... don't give that control away to someone else.

Don't lose your cool, get angry, or fuss; *that's* giving away your control. It also keeps you from being effective as a transformative leader. You'll spend (waste) more time and energy on an ineffective response than you will fixing, replacing, doing over, or moving on to the next, more meaningful, thing.

It is time to stop waiting for someone to save us. It is time to face the truth of our situation – that we're all in this together, that we all have a voice; and figure out how to mobilize the hearts and minds of everyone in our workplaces and communities, Margaret Wheatley and Debbie Frieze.

Transformative leaders know, and do, this with regularity. They run in when others are running away. They see a need or gap and work to resolve or close it. They don't look around for somebody else to save it or close it. Transformative leaders push up their sleeves, put on their boots, and wade into the fray.

If you can't handle a horse without spurs, you have no business riding, Jessica Drummand in *40 Guns.*

People respond most positively to appreciation for their contributions. Study after study reveals that money is *not* the most powerful motivator for effective performance at work, home, or school. It's appreciation! So, why do we continue to throw money at them? Because it's easier!

It's easier than spending time getting to know the man who follows you, learning his strengths, and giving him assignments that fit him. It's easier than figuring out what motivates him and using that to show your appreciation for the work he does. It's easier than learning his areas for improvement and working on a project *with* him to develop those areas, and then expressing your pride when he develops a new skill. It's easier to just do it yourself or give it to someone else when he makes a mistake or doesn't complete a task or project.

Doing things the easy way doesn't bring about any change, shift, modification, or alteration in him or in the organization. Yes, appreciation requires your investment in him. Yes, it requires your time, energy, and possibly resources. Yes, it means that you may not get the results you need quickly. Yes, it means that he will stumble and restart … perhaps several times. And yes, that's what a transformative leader always tries to do!

I am not impressed by your position, title, and money. I am impressed by how you treat people, Oleg Vishnepolsky.

When it is inconvenient, unpopular, out of the norm, and even uncomfortable; transformative leaders are kind, generous, and loving toward others. She thanks the busser in a restaurant. Leaves a *real* tip for the server. Says, "Thank you" or "Good morning" to the building custodian and doorperson. Holds the door for the person coming behind her. Pushes her chair in when she leaves the conference table. Says, "Excuse me," when she bumps into or brushes against the person on the street. She understands that in the great scheme of things, she is no better and no less than any other human she encounters. She knows that her seemingly small gesture can have a ripple effect.

Remember the commercial about Liberty Mutual and taking responsibility for doing the right thing? The first person does something kind for someone else and they, in turn, pay it forward; and so on. It really does work that way. We send little messages out all day, nonverbally, in the way we treat others – especially, when we think no one is watching – because *someone* is always watching. Those messages either impress or disappoint the viewer. Once we disappoint someone, we rarely, if ever, get a second chance with him. He makes up his mind about us in that one brief encounter, and usually tells others; especially if it was negative, he will tell far more people than if the encounter was positive.

What do your actions tell others about you? When I served on the Fort Walton Beach City Council, I had a practice of spending time, once a year, with the employees in every department. It was a wonderful way for me to know what was going on, what they needed, and what issues they had. A bonus was having that extra insight when I had to vote on an agenda item. My decisions were formed based on first-hand knowledge and facts.

During a ride-along with one of our police officers, he told me the story of a fellow Council Member who was stopped for speeding one evening. "When I walked up to his window, he started yelling," the officer said. "'Do you know who you just stopped? I can have your badge,' he yelled at me. Yes, sir, I replied, and you were going 15-miles over the 35-mile speed limit, I told him. Dr. gossom, he yelled at me the whole time I wrote the ticket. I knew it could cost me, but I had a job to do," he continued. "What he did wasn't right," the Officer finished and looked at me. "Thankfully, Chief didn't fire me … (he paused, then grinned) and he (the Council Member) had to pay the ticket. Everyone knows about it, and he doesn't speed in City limits anymore!"

Like I said, it's how you treat people … and what they say about you to others.

Some of us think holding on makes us strong, but sometimes it is letting go,
Herman Hesse.

Just like the art of war is knowing when to engage in battle, it is also knowing when to walk away. Steven Sample, a former president of the University of Southern California calls this, "knowing the hill worth dying on." We work so hard and want so badly to rescue and fix everyone. A good leader knows she can't be rescued and tries anyway; a great leader knows and encourages her to fix the issues; a transformative leader knows and helps her find a better fit.

A reliable way to make people believe in falsehoods is frequent repetition, because familiarity is not easily distinguished from truth. Authoritarian institutions and marketers have always known this fact, Daniel Kahneman. and *Repeat a lie often enough and it becomes the truth,* Joseph Goebbels.

We see this played out in so many arenas – politics, education, business, finance, cultural norms, even pseudoscientific "race" biology. If we push back against the lie, we often get labeled, "radical" socially or "insubordinate" professionally. The truth however, is that unfortunately, the voices of the few who do push back are often overshadowed by the many who believe.

So, what, as transformative leaders, should we do? We keep speaking truth to power. We speak truth to as many as possible, giving them facts. Anywhere we go, however we can, we expose the lie. Sometimes, yes, at great personal, social, and even professional cost. Is it worth it? Only you can answer that question for yourself. Make no mistake though; the people who follow you, trust you, believe in you, will also look to you for truth. They will ask you to tell them if the lie is real or just a lie. You need to be prepared to answer.

If you don't fight for what you love, then you have nothing worth losing, Penny Reid.

I can love you without liking you. I can't like you without loving you though. There are very, *very* few people I don't like. So, for me at least, I won't fight for you unless I like and love you because you're worth the fight and I don't want to lose you or see you lose.

Not everyone will agree with my philosophy. That's okay. I can live with that. At the same time, some of you will think, "You know, that makes a lot of sense" or "I'm the same way." Either way, at your core, unless someone or something is worth it to you, there is no urgency for you to fight for it or them. When they are worthy, those are the battles we wade into, the skirmishes we can't run away from, and the wars that must be won. Those are the times we see someone being bullied or marginalized and we speak up because of our love for humankind or love toward the individual. We care. The issue is worth it. The results will be transformational for everyone involved.

There are four levels of skill development: unconsciously unskilled, which meant you didn't know how much you didn't know and couldn't do; consciously unskilled, which was when you began to be aware of how much you needed to develop; consciously skilled, which was the level at which you started to use what you've trained yourself to do; and, finally, unconsciously skilled, Milton Erickson.

Which things are at your unconsciously skilled level? The things you can do without even thinking about or focusing on? Leadership fits quite nicely on that continuum, I think. Problem solving, visioning, personnel assessment, strategic planning, assignment giving, and all the rest lie somewhere along the scale. Make sure you honestly know where you are with each leadership tool you need in your box so you can consciously work your way toward the unconscious.

This was one of those instances where it was easier to obtain forgiveness than permission. Although right now, I'm questioning the whole forgiveness thing.

Curtis Coggin at Georgia Power, Plant E.I. Hatch taught me this. He hated it when I used it with him though! Confession time. I wasn't always a well-behaved student or child for that matter. Having one of those "innocent" faces let me get away with … a lot.

At school, who made the rude noises while her head was down and it looked like she was busy working when Sister lowered herself into the chair or was standing at the chalkboard? Who convinced her younger cousin to eat tar by telling her it was chocolate? Who would lead the way as she and her cousins snuck out of their bedroom window to flatten nickels on the train tracks? Hand raised. Rarely ever got caught. When I did, I apologized. There was no way I was going to ask for permission! Never lied or outright denied and always, when pressed, told the truth. As you can imagine I spent a lot of time being sent to my room, left with a baby sitter while everyone else went someplace fun, or otherwise being punished (laughing).

Eventually, I settled down, although I still like to shake it up every now and then. The lesson from Curtis was one I had lived my entire life. Like him, it drives me crazy when someone uses it on me!

'Because of how power works,' he says. 'It's a zero-sum game. It's based on making decisions and being able to react to conditions,' S. E. Lund.

When you operate from a mental position of personal power, able to correctly assess and respond to the situation in front of you, there is almost a guaranteed outcome. When your "win" results in a corresponding "loss" it's a zero-sum game. They don't happen often in organizations. Frequently, the loss is greater than the win. You terminate an incompetent employee then have to go through the expense (time and resources) of hiring another. You fail a student, then have to teach him again during the following year or semester when he repeats the grade or class. Sometimes the win is greater than the loss. You return a defective item and find a better one on sale for less than you originally paid. The program that fell through ended up not being necessary to gain the client after all. When your goal is transformation of yourself and others, you won't always have zero-sum victories. Knowing which ones to go after and which ones to let go; knowing which hills to die on and which ones to just blow up; or recognizing when you simply can't shut down the opposition no matter what you do, is hard. Knowing how to read the situation and choosing the best course of action is transformative leadership.

PEOPLE WHO LIVE IN GLASS HOUSES …

self-reflection and vulnerability with others and ourselves

God is the only one who can create something out of nothing. The rest of us must create out of what's already available.

I love this! Drives me nuts when people walk around being arrogant like they created something from nothing ... wrong! We use the tools, resources, talent, and skills we have, yes ... and we don't create from nothing (smh & lol). Everything of value is the result of a transformation. Diamonds from coal; pearls from sand; smartphones from landlines and walkie-talkies; ballpoint pens from quill and ink; chain stores from sole proprietors; universities from Socrates .... What can you create, that is innovative and fresh, from "the way we've always done it" to let those whom you lead, run with? Give them a challenge, as well as the tools, resources, and time to tinker. Then, stand back and let them fly. Transform your organization by transforming the people who work there into creators. The growth and change just may surprise you.

I like your Christ. I do not like your Christians. They are so unlike your Christ, Mohandas Karamchand Gandhi.

I am always amazed at the way some people who profess to be Christians behave toward others. Especially toward those whom they think are not Christian. There are millions of children living in poverty across the globe. There are, still today, places where supposedly well-meaning countries and individuals impose their languages, customs, cultures, and religion upon sovereign nations that already have their own languages, customs, cultures, and religion. When the sovereign nations resist or fight back, it's seen as hostile, savage, and rebellious. Why?

Take almost any industrialized, predominantly Christian, country. There are people who are homeless, living paycheck-to-paycheck, without healthcare, or access to medicine, food, adequate shelter, living wages, or quality education. Does that country invest every possible resource and effort into improving the quality of life for its own citizens? Too many of them do not.

They're halfway around the world, throwing money at wars; relief efforts that amount to little more than dependency-building handouts; trying to … right … impose their own language, customs, culture, and religion on another sovereign nation. Why?

Here's another example. Wasn't Christ the one who said to witness in "Jerusalem [home], *then* to Judea [nation] and Samaria [those in your own country not like you], and to the ends of the earth [other countries]" (Acts 1:8)? Until "home" is right, we can't be effective anywhere else; we just make a mess! It doesn't matter if "home" is a household, extended family, place of worship, school, business, city, state, or nation. As leaders who claim to follow a Christian example, fix what's in front of you *before* you try to fix someone, or someplace, else. Transformative leadership always begins with ourselves, regardless of the beliefs you uphold or practice.

Those who can, do … Those who can do it better, teach, modified from George Bernard Shaw.

For years, I heard the the opposite, "Those who can, do … Those who can't, teach" (George Bernard Shaw). One day, I was thinking about that and it occurred to me that there would be no doctors, economists, entrepreneurs, university presidents, corporate CEOs, or pretty much any type of leader without educators who prepared them to do what they're doing. How extraordinary if you really think about it. An educator taught him how to hold the scalpel. An educator taught her the calculus that lets her determine maximal profit. Without those who teach, those who do … couldn't!

We judge others by their actions and ourselves by our intent, Dwight Morrow. and *There are no facts, only interpretations,* Friedrich Wilhelm Nietzsche. and *If you were them and not you, consider that there is a very good chance that you would behave exactly the same,* Hal Elrod.

This is so important, especially when we are in leadership roles. How often does she look at the actions of another person and decide that he was "good" or "bad" based on observable actions alone ... never considering the circumstances that led to the actions? Yet, when she is confronted with her own actions that caused pain or anger for someone, she defends her actions and expects the other person to forgive because her intent was good. She needs to realize that, unless he is a sociopath, everything that he does, in the moment he does it, makes sense and is the only reasonable course of action available at that moment. Often, days later, or sometimes even seconds later, another alternative, reason, or option becomes crystal clear.

How we interpret the actions of others, not the facts surrounding their actions, usually determines how we respond. Why? Because most of the time, we pass the actions or the facts through our own filters of "the way it *should* be" or "the way I would have done it." Familiar with the, "I can't believe I just did that!" or the, "What was I thinking!" moment? It happens to pretty much everyone .... That's why we should learn to ask, "Why?" when addressing the actions of others, especially of those who choose to follow us. "Tell me why that was the decision you made," or "Talk me through the process you took to get to this point," will get you closer to the intent ... and will help her have a teaching moment. "How could you miss the deadline like this?" will get a defensive and closed-off individual, who isn't likely to commit to following anywhere.

Those who never make mistakes, never make anything ... they don't learn much, either.

I have no idea who should get the credit for this one. There are *so* many variations. Even Yoda said "The greatest teacher, failure is." (smile) The point is that some of my best lessons have come from my biggest mistakes.

One of my most valuable and lasting lessons occurred not long after circumstances forced me to start my first consulting business, Whitt Management Consulting (WMC), when I found myself living in Birmingham, Alabama ... through *yet another* forced circumstance. Settle in, this is a long one!

A former coworker at a major corporation in Birmingham contacted me to ask if I would help him with a Total Quality Management (TQM) initiative for one of the Senior Vice Presidents. I liked "George" and respected his work, so I agreed. (I have a policy that I don't work for or with people I don't like or respect. Thanks Susan Amat!)

George invited me to the planning meeting with the rest of his team, all of whom worked for the corporation. During the meeting, we each took responsibility for segments of the project. I was to develop and facilitate the initial introduction session with the SVP and his Vice Presidents. A woman in George's department would cofacilitate with me, using the material I developed. We were introduced, and although I didn't get strong positive vibes from her, I didn't get any "Stop!" signs either.

"Amy" and I collaborated and reviewed the introductory materials as I developed them; refining and editing so that the current climate and culture of the division could be addressed. It was a major change in the way the division did business; using methods that shouldn't cause the client to throw up barricades. As the day for the introduction session got closer, Amy and I finalized our facilitator notes, participant workbooks, flipcharts, and transparencies. Making sure that everything was aligned and mistake-free.

The day before our session, Amy called me. She sounded, "off," is the best way I could describe it; she asked if I could come earlier than we'd originally planned, so we could go over everything one last time. "Sure," I agreed; and we decided I would arrive an hour earlier than planned. When I got there the next evening, Amy was still "off." She seemed nervous and fidgety. I couldn't pin it down, and chalked it up to the fact that she was new on George's team and that this was her first major project as a new employee. Working to reassure her, I asked if there was anything I could do to make our session stronger.

"Well," Amy began, "John, the Senior Vice President, only respects strength and being challenged." She paused, "I'm still learning TQM and don't know it as well as you do, so I won't be any good at pushing him; especially, if he asks questions I can't answer. Would you be 'bad cop' and let me be 'good cop' during the session?" she asked. Because we only had a few minutes before the clients would start coming in, distracted, I agreed and quickly started adding notes to my facilitator guide. BIG MISTAKE!!

You can imagine what happened, right?!

I was "bad cop," challenging the Senior Vice President to commit to the TQM principles throughout the session. By the time we finished, my stomach was in knots, I was soaked with nervous perspiration, and he was *not* smiling or pleased. When I got home, I had a message on the answering machine informing me that my services were no longer required. I tried to call "Mike," a Vice President I knew in the Division. No answer. I left a message. Called George; no answer. Left him message, explaining. Didn't sleep all night.

The next afternoon, George called me back. Long story short, he said that he understood my explanation and that, had it been anyone else, he could have, "Smoothed things over and it would be okay;" but this SVP *did not* in fact, like to be challenged or questioned. He didn't understand why I would do so. There was nothing he could do. I didn't make excuses or blame Amy. Lesson – hard lesson – learned. Never, *ever* just blindly follow advice given from anyone without first verifying the situation for myself ... *Always* trust my own instincts ... and *always* meet with the client myself.

Years later, working on a different project with the same corporation, I had a chance to talk with the SVP. I apologized. Still didn't blame Amy. Took full responsibility.

By the way, I also found out that Amy had pulled the same thing with someone else and ... got fired.

Garbage in ... compost out.
Full stop!

Still waters run deep and babbling brooks are shallow, Latin Proverb, by attribution.

Another one I'm not certain about the origin of; I just know that Nana (my maternal grandmother) said it to me once. When I was in high school, Nana picked me up and drove me to my school bus stop every morning. The girls' Catholic school I attended was in Cicero, Illinois, outside of my parish, and the closest school bus stop was too far away for me to take the city bus that early in the morning. On that particular day, I got in her car chattering, fussing to Nana about yet another thing her daughter had done that I didn't like.

Nana just drove, more Cherokee stoic than usual; not that I paid any attention! When we got to 79ᵗʰ and Ashland, where she dropped me off, Nana finally looked at me and said, "Still waters run deep and babbling brooks are shallow. Close the door," and turned away. *Huh?* I thought as I closed the car door and watched her drive away. "That makes no sense," I muttered, walking over to the rest of the girls who were waiting for the bus.

All day, I thought about what Nana had said. I looked up the word "still" in the dictionary, "calm, quiet, restful, at peace," were some of the words I remember. Then I looked up "babbling" and found, "noisy, meaningless words." Drop. The. Mic.

So, people who talk a lot, aren't saying anything useful? I thought. *When I'm quiet, I can think, learn, and process. When I'm just chattering, I can't ... and I say things that probably shouldn't be said or that I don't mean.* I decided, that day, to do more listening and less talking. Over the years, I've expanded that lesson into only speaking when I have something meaningful to contribute and becoming more comfortable with silence. It's a lesson that has served me well. Taking that position has kept me from saying things that I would regret, saying things that just made me look important and diminished the value of someone else, and being insensitive or arrogant.

Don't get me wrong, I'm not *always* a "still water," and lots of times I've gotten too caught up in myself and "babbled" like a brook (laughing). Every single time I've forgotten Nana's lesson, I've regretted it or failed as a person ... as a leader. Are you a "still water" leader or a "babbling brook" one? Even more important, which one gives you the best possible chance of initiating growth in yourself and others?

When you discard arrogance, complexity, and a few other things that get in the way, sooner or later you will discover that simple, childlike, and mysterious secret known to those of the Uncarved Block .... Life is Fun, Benjamin Hoff.

I often end a conversation or written communication with the words, "Have fun!" Some people get it ... too many don't.

At their core, children are free of arrogance and posturing. They don't care if their friends are taller, smarter, or have more toys. We, adults, teach them whether those things matter by the way we react to people around us, and them. Children *learn* to be arrogant; they *learn* to body shame, they *learn* to be cruel, and they *learn* to stop having fun. They must be *taught* to build walls of separation between themselves and "others." And that's a shame!

Privilege doesn't mean your life hasn't been hard; it means that the color of your skin, your socioeconomic status, your geographic origin, etc. hasn't contributed to making your life hard, Reggie Shuford, by attribution.

We are a fountain of shimmering contradictions, most of us. Beautiful in the concept, if we're lucky, but frequently tedious or regrettable as we flesh ourselves out, Gregory McGuire.

Just like *The Tao of Pooh* indicates, as we grow, we lose our ability to shimmer, our beauty of simplicity. Transformative leaders see beyond the tedium and regret. They draw out the beauty. They polish to restore the shining glow of all that she is capable of being. Transformative leaders focus on what she could be, less on what she is. Especially when she is eager for, and interested in, growth. As a result, the growth and change allow her to flourish; and she can then bring about transformation in others.

Judge me by the enemies I've made, Franklin Delano Roosevelt.

If those who become my enemies are arrogant, self-centered, act with impunity and meanness toward others … that's a good thing, as far as transformative leaders are concerned. Rather than, "going along," if he stands for what is moral and ethical, and stands against what may be expedient and easy, he can lie down and close his eyes peacefully at night. Knowing that he is leading from a place of true north reassures him … and hopefully, those who choose to follow him as well.

It is the mark of an educated mind to be able to entertain a thought without accepting it, Aristotle. *and Great minds discuss ideas; average minds discuss events; small minds discuss people*, Eleanor Roosevelt.

There was a time when people could have discussions and debates about all kinds of issues without rancor or ugliness. Not sure where that time went; however, I know it isn't true now. Today, it seems that too many people are under the mistaken impression that if you even listen to a differing perspective or viewpoint, that means you automatically agree with it. Personally, I'm sticking with Aristotle and Eleanor … intelligent people can still entertain and discuss divergent thoughts and those who can't or don't are just … well, you get it!

The most important person to forgive is yourself.

Emphasis on "most."

You can fool all the people some of the time, and some of the people all the time, but you cannot fool all the people all the time, Abraham Lincoln.

This sits alongside the quote most frequently attributed to Maya Angelou, "when people show you who they really are, believe them [the first time; don't make them keep showing you]." Thom will wait to trust until he has proof of trustworthiness. I will wait until trust is no longer deserved. Either way, the outcome is the same … no one is ever able to "pretend," one way or the other, for very long.

Usually, a problem, conflict, or crisis reveals the real character. Sometimes it takes longer and sometimes he sees it first, sometimes I do. We always end up with agreement over time. Why? Because my blind spots aren't always his, and vice versa. So, while he may be fooled, I'm not; or we both may be fooled and not for long or always.

As a transformative leader, know your blind spots, have someone close who has different ones, and rely on him or her to guide you out of them.

The question is not what you look at, but what you see, Henry David Thoreau.

We talk a lot about the difference between "hearing" and "listening" not so much about "looking" and "seeing."

While riding as a passenger in a car, I often look out of the window while not seeing anything we pass by. Instead, I'm seeing my thoughts. I may be on my way to give a speech, teach a class or workshop, or visit family. My mind is seeing what I might say, how the room will be set up, whether people will actually come (a frequent one); how we will greet each other, how long my grandson will let me hug him (smile). They aren't on the homes and buildings we pass or the people who live or work in them and their lives.

Other times, usually on vacation or in an unfamiliar area, I see out of the windows. Those are the times I actually notice the differences in architecture, geography, see the dress styles of the people, pay attention to the interactions between groups and couples. I learn things during those moments. I see a new way to wear a scarf. Learn about a mannerism to adopt or drop. Understand the values and culture of other people. I am transformed by what I see. There is something for me to "take away" from those glimpses into the lives of others.

The same is true in leadership. How often do we merely look at those we are leading, not really seeing them? Looking at and not seeing the distress on her face or the worry in his eyes? Usually it's because our focus is inward. In order to *see*, we can't be thinking about or focusing on ourselves; instead, we need to be thinking about the person in front of us. Asking what she needs to be successful or how we can provide what he lacks. That's when the transformational opportunity is present. When we see.

Human beings are flawed.

How I wish we weren't! What an incredible growing, changing, improving world this would be if we had no flaws. We would all consistently choose the best for ourselves and others; no mistakes, no course corrections, no do-overs required. Everything we did would be the best thing for every situation.

Unfortunately, we are flawed. We are human not divine, no matter how much some of us imagine differently! So, what does that mean for our ability to lead effectively? How can we cause transformation in ourselves and those who follow us? How do we ensure that the vision is worthy, the goals are the best ones to get us "there;" the values we live by are honorable and just? We don't. Which is why it is so very important that we allow others to point out the flaws we carry with us.

We need a mentor who will help us course-correct. We need followers who have the freedom and security to point out the things we don't see. We need grace and humility to listen to them when they do.

Your assumptions are your windows on the world. Scrub them off every once in a while, or the light won't come in, Isaac Asimov.

When the debate is lost, slander becomes the tool of the loser, Socrates, by attribution.

Socrates never wrote his thoughts on morality, ethics, and philosophy. Instead, we have accounts of his teaching, primarily documented by Plato and Xenophon. Additionally, there is nothing in the writings of Plato or Xenophon to validate attribution of this quote to Socrates. So why did I include it? Because from the first time I heard it (around 2009 or 2010), the quote stuck with and transformed me, regardless of who actually said it first.

Unlike the past, today we have so many ways to discuss and debate issues. The standbys of newspaper, magazine, television, and radio were joined by Facebook, Twitter, LinkedIn, and Instagram. They have been joined by Snapchat, TikTok, Tumblr, Kik, Reddit, MeWe, and countless others. All of which can be used to discuss and debate points of view and perspectives. Like any other technology … from a simple pencil to a powerful supercomputer, they can also be used to slander when intellect falls short.

Children are cyberbullied by their peers. Politicians slander their opponents in ads and posts. Former friends slander each other on social media platforms in a bid to turn other friends to their "side." Spouses slander spouses in conversations with work colleagues. Students slander their schools and teachers in online, anonymous evaluations. Employees and customers slander businesses online. All because they don't have, or won't take, the time to gather intellectual capital for debate and discussion.

My aunt said something to me when I was a new teenager, feeling full of myself and "adult" when I said a curse word in her presence. "Only ignorant people use words like that, joyce. They're either too lazy or too stupid to use intelligent alternatives." I've *never* forgotten and am often reminded when someone resorts to slander or profanity because they can't formulate a well-reasoned debate or discussion point.

I will not let anyone walk through my mind with their dirty feet, Mohandas Karamchand Gandhi.

This one is so important to pass along to anyone who trusts and follows you. Why do we ever allow the grumblers, snipers, whiners, and complainers to have space in our brains? Turn them off, shut them down, walk away.

To be trusted is a bigger compliment than being loved, George MacDonald.

If Thom tells me where he's going, I know that it's true. He has my trust. Yes, I also love him … he named Best Gurl, inc. after me! More important, at least to me, I implicitly trust him.

If Emily (The Best Gurl Communicator) tells me that she has scheduled the Social Media posts for the month, I believe her because I trust her. If Kimberly (The Best Gurl Researcher) tells me that she couldn't get some information from a source, I believe her because I trust her. If Dixson tells me that he sent a card in the mail, I believe him because I trust him.

I love all of them. They love me. I also trust all of them. As a friend, wife, mother, and leader, it's up to me to make sure they also trust me. Otherwise, they won't follow me and I'll have no opportunity to be transformative in their lives. That would be a shame; for them, and especially for me.

To be left alone and face to face with my own crime, had been just retribution, Henry Wadsworth Longfellow.

Faced with the reality of the destruction caused by her actions, Longfellow has Pandora speak these words to her creator, Epimetheus, when he confronts her.

Words written by a poet describing Greek mythology that still have relevance today. Who among us has ever wished that we could run away from facing the evidence of what our actions brought about? Nothing on the scale of Pandora letting all of the evils out into the world, certainly; however, things that impact the lives of those we care about, lead, and love ... for sure. Being "face to face" with our actions can be worse than suffering punishment for them and can have an even more powerful effect.

When we were about 9 and 10, David, Steve (my cousin-brothers), and I were given permission to go to the movie ... don't remember what we were going to see, and it doesn't matter. What does matter is two things. First, we were going to take the makings of slingshots so that we could make them in the theater and hide them in our jackets, because of course we weren't supposed to have them, much less make them. Second, Uncle Cal (their dad) and Mommy made us take their eight-year-old sister with us (groan). All went well until halfway into the second movie. Slingshots were made, she didn't know we had them (otherwise she would tell on us) and popcorn lasted into the second show. Then some boys we knew, who were sitting in front of us, started throwing candy and popcorn at the screen and talking back to the film at the end of the movie. Could we have gone to tell the manager of the theatre? Sure! But, we had these great slingshots to try out and they were going to be walking in our direction on the way home. Perfect!

We let them leave first, saving the last of our candy and gathering some pebbles as we got outside. Then, the chase was on! Shooting candy and pebbles, we chased them for several blocks, laughing and practicing our aim; all the way to ... wait, that car looks familiar and so does ... shoot! Sitting in his navy-blue Buick across the street on Sangamon was Uncle Cal. Slingshots got tossed into the grass at Oakdale Park, innocence plastered quickly on our faces. This was good, this was going to be ... wait, where was ... we looked at each other, then turned to look behind us ... waaaaaaayyyyy behind us and here she came, running, falling, and crying; their sister. Making "shhhh" and "be quiet" noises, we waited for her to catch up, tried to wipe her up and crossed the street to his car. Opening the door, we chattered, acting like all was fine and we'd done nothing wrong. Silence.

Back to the house. Silence. We walked inside and sat on the couch, waiting for our consequences. Silence. We heard voices in the kitchen and dining room, no one ever called us to dinner and we didn't move. Silence. Hours later, Mommy came into the living room, called my name and we left to go home. Silence. Uncle Cal never did say or do anything to me or to my cousins. It was a horrible and just retribution. Steve and I talk about it every now and then, usually when we go to a movie. We've never forgotten. We never did it again. Lesson learned. Thanks, Uncle Cal.

It's About the Journey ...
Not the Destination
shifting focus and being intentional

Be who you are so that you can do what you should and you will have what you need.

This one perfectly describes my philosophy about work. I've also read,

Do what you love and the money will follow.

Same principle.

Do you look forward to what you do every day? Can you even imagine spending your time doing anything else? If your answers aren't a resounding, "Yes," and "No," then you're not being who you are or doing what you should. You're just going through the motions.

Remember, the goal isn't to get to some arbitrary endpoint; the goal is the path you take, the choices made, and the transformations you leave behind. If what you're doing along the journey isn't what fulfills you and those you're doing it for or with, could it be possible that it isn't what you should be doing? Are you just going through the motions? If so, it's very likely that everyone around you knows it; they aren't receiving what they should from you *and* you're in the way of the person who *can* give them what *they* need on their journey.

Make haste slowly, Kikkoman Motto.

Advance and grow, while doing so with tremendous thought and care, is the history and future of the Kikkoman legacy. Don't be afraid to make quick decisions that are based on strategy and vision. Sometimes you need to decide quickly.

The mark of great transformative leadership is not hesitating when a decision is needed. Those who follow you have learned that your decisions aren't made in a vacuum, and will work hard to carry them out. They're ready for the coming change because they believe in the vision you have, the strategy that you've plotted, and the tasks they have identified; and they're ready to create a new path into the future. Your decisions always result in change. For you. For the people you're leading. So, make haste slowly and just go forth!

Do I really want to let this event ruin my day? Jerry Ross.

If you've ever lived in a place where it snows, or even if you've seen photographs, think about seeing freshly fallen snow covering everything. It's on the tree limbs, covers the dormant grass, makes sidewalks and even streets disappear. Cars and other vehicles look like they have on blankets. What a beautiful and breathtaking sight! Nothing matches the pristine beauty of, and nothing looks quite like, a snow-covered landscape ... until you remember that you need to go out in it!

Maybe you need to go to work, your place of worship, drop children at school, or check on a homebound friend or relative. You grumble, thinking about shoveling the sidewalk or driveway to use your car. Wiping off or scraping windshields or cleaning stairs. "Stupid snow," you might mutter. Then, after layering up against the cold, still grumpy and complaining, you open the door, awestruck at the wonder of the silence. It's like the whole world is breathless. Stillness completely blankets everything, just like the snow. Stepping out into this perfect winter wonderland, you scoop up a handful, marring the once pristine landscape, and form a snowball. You hurl it toward a tree. You're tempted to lie on the ground to make a snow angel, like you did as a child. Shaking your head at the irony, you get to work, glancing behind to realize that what once was perfect, now bears witness to your presence. Before you there is perfection, and forward you go. Realizing that what, at first, was an irritating mess is really a beautiful way to begin your day.

If you can't see it you can't be it, modified from Marian Wright Edelman. and *Who I am being is more important than what I am doing, Daily Word,* 30 December 2019.

What a great thought for the end of my year! I grew up learning to set goals, and having a plan for achieving them. As an adult, I learned that was called "strategic planning." When I was a child, all I knew was that every year in September when school started, I had to write down the three or four things I wanted to do and how I would do them. At first, they were simple things like, not get a low grade for conduct on my report card; successfully doing a pirouette in ballet; playing my piano recital piece without mistakes; riding Cindy (my horse) without a training lead; or not being sent to my room at least once every day!

I wrote my goals on a piece of paper and added the things I needed to do in order to make them happen (tasks/actions). How long I would practice piano or ballet each day; keeping track on my calendar when I practiced to have a good seat, the days I was sent to my room, or got a phone call or note sent home. That was where I focused. Learning to visualize my goals through the actions I would take, or not take, during the year, months, and days. Most of the time, when school ended in June and I reviewed my goals and progress, I'd successfully completed all of them … well, all except being sent to my room! What a great feeling it was! Seeing myself successful in September and being successful in June.

Now, every year, when I sit down at my desk in January and think about my goals for the coming year, I also think about what I had become during the ending one. My goals are usually focused on who I am becoming as a person. Every year, I spend time looking back over the year at my accomplishments and shortcomings and purposefully decide what aspects of my character I will focus on during the new year.

Seeing and Being is a huge part of the life journey, regardless of what you call it or whether you start on your birthday, beginning of the school year, the new year, or just a random day. The important thing is that transformation first requires you to See the possible before you can Be the reality. Those who follow you need to learn that lesson as well.

There is such great beauty in loving someone else as fully and completely as possible.

Especially those who are on the journey with you. Love deeply. Live fully. Enjoy every single moment with them!

It's not just about living forever; the trick is living with yourself forever, Captain Teague in *Pirates of the Caribbean: Dead Man's Chest*

... and enjoying who you are, what you do, whom you're with, where you are going ... forever! Live the life you would live as though you have forever to live it. Make sure it's a life worth living ... forever; otherwise, make a list of what you would change and start the transformation – right now, today. At home. At work. At life!

I don't know if we each have a destiny, or if we're floating around on a breeze, accidental like. I think maybe, it's a little of both, Forrest Gump.

For transformative leaders, it's always both. Sometimes, along our life journey, we float along. Employees or other followers are implementing the strategy, working the plan; and we're free to float. Free to soar up to 20,000 or 40,000 feet and look out over the future of possibility. Free to envision the next adventure, conquest, or achievement. Until we can see it on the breeze. Visualizing the future, until it becomes clear what we should lead others toward.

We glide back down to describe the future. Explain the "what" and "why." Work with those who follow us to craft the "how" of getting there. Forming a new strategy and plan. Making sure they know how to do the new tasks and activities. Providing the best possible environment for success. Getting the resources and tools they will need for development and implementation. Figuring out who doesn't want to go in the new direction and helping them find a place where they can be successful.

Once everyone and everything is in place and moving forward, up you go; floating again in search of the next future. Leading the way toward transformation and growth.

Do what you believe and believe what you do, Dixson Michael Gossom.

My son is counted among the wisest people I know. He is one of those, "still waters" that Nana talked about. He doesn't say much; sometimes, to the frustration of those who follow or work beside him. Yet, when he has something to say, it adds value.

Dixson is one of those people you can count on to only do what he believes in. You may not understand, or even believe in the same thing(s) he does; at the same time, you will always know that if he is doing it, he believes in it. That, alone, demands respect. He's always been that way.

As a child, Dixson would think about what he was being asked to do or the direction he was told to go. Without a lot of fussing or arguing, he would either do it … or not. Raising him, leading him, I learned a valuable leadership lesson. If I gave him the knowledge, skills, tools, resources, and environment, only he could decide whether to follow. Sometimes, he did and sometimes he didn't. When he didn't, Dixson would accept the consequences; whatever they were, and he *still* wouldn't do whatever it was. (Wonder where he got *that* from?!)

It was the best possible preparation for me in transformational leadership. I could envision all the goals and strategies I wanted; if no one wanted to follow, it wouldn't be achieved. If people don't believe, they won't do. Just like my son.

You can't go back and change the beginning, but you can start where you are and change the ending, C.S. Lewis.

How many times in the course of your life have you thought, "If only …?" Somehow, it doesn't matter how many years we've lived or worked, we all seem to have at least one of those thoughts, maybe more.

Although I can't do anything about changing the personal ending for those who choose to follow me, I've always tried to do something about the work environment they have. I don't ever want him to wish he had never taken the job. I want him to feel that the time is well spent and the growth is positive when the ending comes and it's time for him to move on towards "What's Next?" for him. I can decide to create an environment of focusing as much on his journey as I do on the journey of the organization. After all, there is no organization without the people.

We are what we repeatedly tell ourselves. We become our own story. and *Whether you think you can or think you can't, you're right,* Henry Ford.

Every time I see, or think about, this saying, the song about the ant and the rubber tree pops into my head (laughing). Don't know or remember it?

> *Just what makes that little old ant*
> *Think he'll move that rubber tree plant*
> *Anyone knows an ant, can't*
> *Move a rubber tree plant*
> *But he's got high hopes*
> *He's got high hopes*
> *He's got high apple pie*

In the sky hopes
So any time your gettin' low
'Stead of lettin' go
Just remember that ant
Oops, there goes another rubber tree plant
Jimmy Van Heusen, Sammy Cahn

High hopes are what keep me going when I feel defeated, tired, or discouraged. I remember the ant who moved all those rubber tree plants and remind myself of the bridges I've already built so I could cross the rivers and canyons of my life. I think about the darkest and most difficult days, weeks, months, and sometimes years that I have survived and move forward in the telling of my story.

Each obstacle overcome, each tragedy survived, every path I've had to clear, has changed me. Strengthened me. Forged me ever closer to steel. As it has for those who follow me.

Sometimes, she needs you to remind her of where she has been and how she has thrived. Sometimes, he needs encouragement to just keep going. When they do, remind her; encourage him; give them what they need; refocus their attention on the goal … and hum the rubber tree song for yourself.

The chapters of life are sometimes painful and brutal. And the only one who can commiserate with you in the vat of loneliness is the voice in your head reminding you of the one thing you most believe in.

Thom and I have what he calls, "adventures." Whether you call them chapters, adventures, stages, passages … they all add up to the same thing … life. Sometimes, our individual adventures have been anything but enjoyable. The loss of people we know and love; the illness of family and friends; relationship tears and fractures; job and career endings. Disappointments, frustrations, and sorrow have woven their way into our lives, as individuals and as a couple.

Throughout all our adventures, however, one constant always remains. What we believe in, and our faith in the ultimate outcome, sustains us. Our inner voices that remind us who we are and what we have already survived keep us moving forward during those dark and lonely times.

We each deal with those periods differently. Thom talks things through and I internalize the processing. As a couple, we allow the other to process as they will, without judgement or criticism. Being supportive in the way the other needs, not imposing our own way.

For me, as I process the loss and what it means for my life going forward; as I struggle through the daily realization of a serious illness and the changes it impacts on my life; as I privately cry over a relationship that may be forever gone, or figure out what I will do next when a job or client goes away; he waits until I am ready to listen, to hear, to visualize the continuation of the adventure that is our lives.

Everyone needs the space and freedom to hear the voice in their head and respond to it in their own way. As a transformative leader, I must also give that freedom to those around me. To let Thom talk. To let Dixson process. To listen and give insight to Sissy. To wait until Joanna is ready. To give Judy reassurance. To really hear beneath the words that Rones says. To not push Emily, to reach out or not reach out to Linda or Sharon. Help connect the dots for Crystal, Max, Kat, or Alex. Knowing what each person needs from me as he or she navigates through the murky roiling waters and being there to celebrate when the water is once again clear and calm … that is my gift to them. It's the gift you can and should give to those who follow you along the journey.

I'm not lost for I know where I am. But however, where I am may be lost, A.A. Milne.

As *anyone* who really knows me can tell you, I love Winnie the Pooh, and by association, A.A. Milne. Pooh is such a model for transformative leadership! Unassuming. Humble. Honest. Generous about everything except honey. Focused (when it comes to honey and getting more of it). Dependable. I could go on and on. This quote is one of my favorites by Pooh and is so appropriate for transformative leadership.

There are so many times I have known exactly where I was on the path to achieving a goal or vision with those who were following me. At the same time, I absolutely knew that where we were wasn't where we should have been. We weren't "lost;" where we were *was* "lost." We weren't where we should be and I had no idea how to get there.

Those were the times that humility came into play. Admitting to those who were following that we were off-track. Going in the wrong direction. On an unfamiliar path. Asking for their help in figuring out either how to get back to where we should be or for help charting a new course from where we were.

The important lesson is in the acknowledgement. Those who are following you have insight. They have experience … shared and individual. So, when you're not "lost" yet *where* you are *is* "lost," ask for help. If you truly are a transformative leader, it will gladly be given to you and the journey will continue. If you're not; well, that's a different lesson.

It is good to have an end to journey toward; but it is the journey that matters most, in the end, Ernest Hemingway.

When she was younger, "Toni" was always anxious to get to "what's next." She couldn't wait to start kindergarten, then she couldn't wait to get out of elementary and into middle school. After that, she couldn't wait for high school and leaving home for college; then graduating and pursuing her love of and talent for music. Along the way, she was told to enjoy where she was ... kindergarten and meeting life-long friends; elementary and gaining the gifts of reading and problem solving; middle and high school opportunities to perform and hone her craft. While at one of the best universities in the country for music, she was encouraged to build relationships, tryout for every opportunity, do internships during the summers, and lay a foundation for her future.

Today, Toni is an unhappy, frustrated wife and mother who never realized her potential because her focus was on the end. She ignored, or didn't take advantage of, the invaluable opportunities that came along the journey because she was focused on "getting there." The sad reality is that she is like many others who miss the doors and windows that will enrich and enhance the road-trip journey in favor of jumping on the expressway and zipping toward the exit.

Enjoying, and paying attention along, the journey would have made a critical difference in where Toni ultimately ended up. That friend she lost contact with from high school is now an assistant producer at a major broadcasting and communications company. A college roommate she couldn't wait to get away from did a summer internship at one of the top music streaming platforms and now has the job of finding new talent. The professor who asked her to be his teaching assistant in her Junior year, just got tapped as Dean of the Music College and has multiple faculty positions to fill. Doors, windows, opportunities, all missed; all would have taken Toni where she wanted to go as a musician, singer, and songwriter.

No matter how far you travel, you can never get away from yourself, Haruki Murakami.

I am always with me. On every journey, in every adventure. The question is, do I like and love my constant traveling companion? If "yes," travel on and earn. If "no," what do I need to change or gain before I should move forward?

In a day, when you don't come across any problems — you can be sure that you are travelling in a wrong path, Swami Vivekananda.

Okay, so let me just start by saying I *know* I'm on the right path!

At the beginning of every week, either Sunday or Monday, Thom and I say to each other, "Let's see what this week brings," because we know that there will be a bump, glitch, surprise, disappointment, or issue to deal with. Does it make us swerve off path? Sometimes. Does it strengthen and harden our resolve that we're on the right path? Always.

Problems don't always indicate that you're not doing what is best or that you're heading in a direction you shouldn't. Most of the time, they're an opportunity to refine the goal; take an alternate route; draw your attention to a new window of opportunity. A chance to slow you down and allow you to refocus before continuing.

Life is not a dress rehearsal, Rose Tremain.

Just like Seeing and Being, this life isn't a "practice run," it's the only shot we get. We have just one opportunity to make a difference, create a legacy, and leave our mark on the world. Don't waste it! Don't put off what you can attempt today, now, by saying you'll try next year or after you retire. You may not have next year. What if you don't make it to retirement? Everything you were meant to do and should do to make a contribution to the world will be lost … forever. Your life *is* your performance; not your dress rehearsal. Don't be like "Everybody" and assume that "Somebody" will do it; or that

"Anybody" else can do it; because "Nobody" except you will accomplish *your* life's purpose. You're the only person who can do what you're supposed to do. There is no one else.

NOT SO FAMOUS LAST WORDS

Like millions of people, I've watched the movie *Wizard of Oz* since I was a very young girl. "Wait. What does this have to do with transformative leadership?" you ask …. "Just go with it!"

Also like many, I've read all the L. Frank Baum books. As an adult, I've read *The Wicked Years* book series by Gregory Maguire and have seen the Broadway play adaptation of *Wicked* twice, once with Myko and once with Thom. That either makes me a huge fan or slightly obsessed! Eh, a little of both, actually. I always cried near the end of *Wizard of Oz*, long before Dorothy ever made it back to Kansas.

I learned a lot about transformational leadership and people from the characters in the film, books (both sets), and musical. Recently, I discovered a great article by Sharon Kruse and Sandra Spickard Prettyman that also deals with leadership. Here's what I have learned from the collective "Ozian" tales.

The Wizard was the kind of leader who pretends to be more than he is, while using others to do the things he's afraid and incapable of doing himself. Namely, having Dorothy kill the Witch of the West. He misused transformative leadership to change his appearance and behaviors to compensate for his fear and has no real ability; just trinkets he used to keep others distracted or complacent. Remember that in the film, the Wizard was also the gatekeeper, carriage driver, and guard. He proclaimed himself to be "the great and powerful," (Kruse & Prettyman) but did nothing about providing solutions for the social and cultural injustice present in the *Wicked* books and play. In fact, this type of leader will turn popular opinion against those who point out his shortcomings in an effort to destroy credibility … (*Wicked*). Just like his balloon, the Wizard is the kind of leader who is full of hot air with no substance.

Glinda/Galinda is the kind of leader who uses appearance and charm to gain "position and power," (Kruse & Prettyman). She used popularity (*Wicked*) as a way to establish and maintain her status, while never really doing more than building a "power base" through charming others. In the film, Glinda didn't go take the shoes for herself, she charmed Dorothy into doing it for her. Then, because she wanted the Witch of the West gone to solidify her position as the only Witch in Oz, she "neglected" to tell Dorothy that the shoes could immediately take her home. Again, Glinda used her appearance, little girl voice, and popularity with the Munchkins to convince Dorothy to travel to Oz for help when she could have helped her right then. Glinda/Galinda is the kind of leader who is always, always about maintaining status and appearance … doesn't matter that nothing is accomplished and people sometimes get hurt.

That brings me to Dorothy. Ugh (my least favorite character)! She led by manipulating others. The Scarecrow was manipulated into doing all the planning. Getting from Munchkinland to Oz, getting to the Witch's castle, and figuring out that Glinda could help Dorothy after the Wizard took off. The Tin Man was manipulated into sacrificing himself to keep her safe. Putting out the fire, rusting in the poppy field, and fighting off the Winkie soldiers. The Lion, of course, was manipulated because of his size and strength. I think Dorothy, as a leader, is most dangerous because she manipulates people into being committed to the goal, then leaves behind the very ones who got her "there" once the goal is reached.

Last, and most important to me, is the Witch of the West/Elphaba. She represents the kind of transformative leader who doesn't seek attention or fame, doesn't really "fit in" with the other leaders, and refuses to remain silent about the injustice or oppression of others. She is an "outsider," (Kruse & Prettyman) and eventually, the Witch of the West/Elphaba learns to like it that way because of the changes for good that she ultimately brings about.

The thing is, the Witch of the West/Elphaba is, like too many transformative leaders, vilified by those who are in power and loved by those who are oppressed. Frequently, she is on the receiving end of plans to "bring her down," (Kruse & Prettyman). She stepped into a leadership role, not because she sought power and status, or had her own agenda, but to meet a present and persistent need. As it happens all too often, the Witch of the West/Elphaba's transformative approach achieves the end of the injustice or oppression only to be brought down herself for her effort.

True transformative leaders use the tools and resources, vision and strategies, and lessons and words she has learned, to bring about lasting improvements and change in the lives of others and in herself.

Do I read too much into the books, movie, and play about the Witch of the West/Elphaba? Maybe. Then again, there are lessons everywhere if we pay attention, which is how this book came about. Think about the leaders you know. I'll bet you could categorize each into one or more of these four types if you are honest. Which ones really are transformative? Which ones work to bring out the best in others? Which ones make sacrifices so that their followers can go forward, even if it means going without them? They are the unconventional, transformative leaders we *want* to follow.

So, when did I cry during the movie, books, and play? I cried when the Witch of the West/Elphaba was "liquified," of course! Why cry over the Witch? Well, if someone killed your sibling, stole your inheritance, then acted like **you** were the wicked one … you'd be angry and go after them too! Unconventional, transformative leadership comes in many forms. Hopefully, the form you choose will bring about change that is for the good!

ABOUT THE AUTHOR

Born in Chicago, Dr. joyce gillie gossom has spent her life going against the grain. At the age of 16, she felt so connected to the poetry and style of e.e. cummings that her mother let joyce legally change her name to all lowercase letters, which is frequently met with resistance by those who insist on "correcting" it.

joyce's more than 40 years of professional experience range from special education teacher to higher education administrator; mid-level manager to leadership coach; and from organizational consultant to elected official. Throughout her career, she has almost always served as an active member or officer with civic, professional, and community organizations.

Currently, joyce serves as The Princess (President) of Best Gurl, inc. a consulting company providing customized solutions for corporations, education, and non-profits that lead to improved performance. She is the author of *Why Are They Following Me?: A Guide to Effective Leadership* and *What Am I Supposed to Say?: An Unconventional Guide to Transformative Leadership*.

joyce and her husband live in Fort Walton Beach, Florida and they have one son. She likes butterflies, the colors purple and yellow, Winnie the Pooh, The Wicked Witch/Elphaba, and large bodies of water.

Leave a Review: https://buff.ly/3feC1sO
Facebook: https://www.facebook.com/joyce.gillie.gossom
Goodreads: https://buff.ly/2Ss1PYA
Linked In: https://www.linkedin.com/in/dr-joyce-gillie-gossom/
Twitter: https://twitter.com/jggossom57

CPSIA information can be obtained
at www.ICGtesting.com
Printed in the USA
LVHW050150080221
678682LV00012B/826

9 780989 086578